The Author

STEPHEN LEACOCK was born in Swanmore, Hampshire, England, in 1869. His family emigrated to Canada in 1876 and settled on a farm north of Toronto. Educated at Upper Canada College and the University of Toronto, Leacock pursued graduate studies in economics at the University of Chicago, where he studied under Thorstein Veblen.

Even before he completed his doctorate, Leacock accepted a position as sessional lecturer in political science and economics at McGill University. When he received his Ph.D. in 1903, he was appointed to the full position of lecturer. From 1908 until his retirement in 1936, he chaired the Department of Political Science and Economics.

Leacock's most profitable book was his textbook, *Elements of Political Science*, which was translated into seventeen languages. The author of nineteen books and countless articles on economics, history, and political science, Leacock turned to the writing of humour as his beloved avocation. His first collection of comic stories, *Literary Lapses*, appeared in 1910, and from that time until his death he published a volume of humour almost every year.

Leacock also wrote popular biographies of his two favourite writers, Mark Twain and Charles Dickens. At the time of his death, he left four completed chapters of what was to have been his autobiography. These were published posthumously under the title *The Boy I Left Behind Me*.

Stephen Leacock died in Toronto, Ontario, in 1944.

THE NEW CANADIAN LIBRARY

General Editor: David Staines

Stephen Leacock

MY FINANCIAL CAREER

and Other Follies

Selected and
with an Afterword by David Staines

M&S

Canadian Cataloguing in Publication Data

Leacock, Stephen, 1869-1944
My financial career and other follies

(New Canadian library)
Includes bibliographical references.
ISBN 0-7710-9892-8

I. Title.   II. Series.

PS8523.E15M9 1993   C813'.54   C93-093796-1
PR9199.2.L42M9 1993

Series design by T.M. Craan
Cover design by Andrew Skuja
Typesetting by M&S, Toronto
The support of the Government of Ontario through the Ministry of
Culture and Communications is acknowledged.

Printed and bound in Canada by Webcom Ltd.

McClelland & Stewart Inc.
The Canadian Publishers
481 University Avenue
Toronto, Ontario
M5G 2E9

Contents

Acknowledgements

The year printed at the end of each story indicates its original date of publication. Stephen Leacock sometimes made minor revisions to his stories between their serial publication and their inclusion in one of his books. In such instances I have reprinted the volume rather than the serial version: "My Financial Career" and "The Awful Fate of Melpomenus Jones" (*Literary Lapses* 1910); "Gertrude the Governess: or, Simple Seventeen" (*Nonsense Novels* 1911); "The Marine Excursion of the Knights of Pythias" (*Sunshine Sketches of a Little Town* 1912); "The Dentist and the Gas" (*Behind the Beyond and Other Contributions to Human Knowledge* 1913); "The Love Story of Mr. Peter Spillikins" (*Arcadian Adventures with the Idle Rich* 1914); "The Reading Public: A Book Store Study" (*Moonbeams from the Larger Lunacy* 1915); "The Snoopopaths or Fifty Stories in One" and "Humour As I See It" (*Further Foolishness: Sketches and Satires on the Follies of the Day* 1916); "My Revelations as a Spy" and "Personal Adventures in the Spirit World" (*Frenzied Fiction* 1918); "War and Peace at the Galaxy Club" (*The Hohenzollerns in America; With the Bolsheviks in Berlin, and Other Impossibilities* 1919); "Buggam Grange: A Good Old Ghost Story" (*Winsome Winnie and Other New Nonsense Novels* 1920); "How We Kept Mother's Day" (*Winnowed Wisdom* 1926); "Old Junk and New

Money" and "A Lesson on the Links" (*Short Circuits* 1928);
"Fifty Cents' Worth" (*The Iron Man and The Tin Woman and
Other Futurities* 1929); "The Perfect Optimist" and "Ho for
Happiness" (*The Dry Pickwick and Other Incongruities* 1932);
"My Remarkable Uncle" and "The Saving Grace of Humour"
(*My Remarkable Uncle and Other Sketches* 1942); "Good News!
A New Party!" (*Happy Stories Just to Laugh At* 1943).

D.S.

My Financial Career

W<small>HEN I GO</small> into a bank I get rattled. The clerks rattle me; the wickets rattle me; the sight of the money rattles me; everything rattles me.

The moment I cross the threshold of a bank and attempt to transact business there, I become an irresponsible idiot.

I knew this beforehand, but my salary had been raised to fifty dollars a month and I felt that the bank was the only place for it.

So I shambled in and looked timidly round at the clerks. I had an idea that a person about to open an account must needs consult the manager.

I went up to a wicket marked "Accountant." The accountant was a tall, cool devil. The very sight of him rattled me. My voice was sepulchral.

"Can I see the manager?" I said, and added solemnly, "alone." I don't know why I said "alone."

"Certainly," said the accountant, and fetched him.

The manager was a grave, calm man. I held my fifty-six dollars clutched in a crumpled ball in my pocket.

"Are you the manager?" I said. God knows I didn't doubt it.

"Yes," he said.

"Can I see you," I asked, "alone?" I didn't want to say "alone" again, but without it the thing seemed self-evident.

The manager looked at me in some alarm. He felt that I had an awful secret to reveal.

"Come in here," he said, and led the way to a private room. He turned the key in the lock.

"We are safe from interruption here," he said. "Sit down."

We both sat down and looked at each other. I found no voice to speak.

"You are one of Pinkerton's men, I presume," he said.

He had gathered from my mysterious manner that I was a detective. I knew what he was thinking, and it made me worse.

"No, not from Pinkerton's," I said, seeming to imply that I came from a rival agency.

"To tell the truth," I went on, as if I had been prompted to lie about it, "I am not a detective at all. I have come to open an account. I intend to keep all my money in this bank."

The manager looked relieved but still serious; he concluded now that I was a son of Baron Rothschild or a young Gould.

"A large account, I suppose," he said.

"Fairly large," I whispered. "I propose to deposit fifty-six dollars now and fifty dollars a month regularly."

The manager got up and opened the door. He called to the accountant.

"Mr. Montgomery," he said unkindly loud, "this gentleman is opening an account, he will deposit fifty-six dollars. Good morning."

I rose.

A big iron door stood open at the side of the room.

"Good morning," I said, and stepped into the safe.

"Come out," said the manager coldly, and showed me the other way.

I went up to the accountant's wicket and poked the ball of money at him with a quick convulsive movement as if I were doing a conjuring trick.

My face was ghastly pale.

"Here," I said, "deposit it." The tone of the words seemed to mean, "Let us do this painful thing while the fit is on us."

He took the money and gave it to another clerk.

He made me write the sum on a slip and sign my name in a book. I no longer knew what I was doing. The bank swam before my eyes.

"Is it deposited?" I asked in a hollow, vibrating voice.

"It is," said the accountant.

"Then I want to draw a cheque."

My idea was to draw out six dollars of it for present use. Someone gave me a cheque-book through a wicket and someone else began telling me how to write it out. The people in the bank had the impression that I was an invalid millionaire. I wrote something on the cheque and thrust it in at the clerk. He looked at it.

"What! are you drawing it all out again?" he asked in surprise. Then I realised that I had written fifty-six instead of six. I was too far gone to reason now. I had a feeling that it was impossible to explain the thing. All the clerks had stopped writing to look at me.

Reckless with misery, I made a plunge.

"Yes, the whole thing."

"You withdraw your money from the bank?"

"Every cent of it."

"Are you not going to deposit any more?" said the clerk, astonished.

"Never."

An idiot hope struck me that they might think something had insulted me while I was writing the cheque and that I had changed my mind. I made a wretched attempt to look like a man with a fearfully quick temper.

The clerk prepared to pay the money.

"How will you have it?" he said.

"What?"

"How will you have it?"

"Oh" – I caught his meaning and answered without even trying to think – "in fifties."

He gave me a fifty-dollar bill.

"And the six?" he asked dryly.

"In sixes," I said.

He gave it me and I rushed out.

As the big door swung behind me I caught the echo of a roar of laughter that went up to the ceiling of the bank. Since then I bank no more. I keep my money in cash in my trousers pocket and my savings in silver dollars in a sock.

(1895)

The Awful Fate of Melpomenus Jones

SOME PEOPLE – not you nor I, because we are so awfully self-possessed – but some people, find great difficulty in saying good-bye when making a call or spending the evening. As the moment draws near when the visitor feels that he is fairly entitled to go away he rises and says abruptly, "Well, I think I . . ." Then the people say, "Oh, must you go now? Surely it's early yet!" And a pitiful struggle ensues.

I think the saddest case of this kind of thing that I ever knew was that of my poor friend Melpomenus Jones, a curate – such a dear young man, and only twenty-three! He simply couldn't get away from people. He was too modest to tell a lie, and too religious to wish to appear rude. Now it happened that he went to call on some friends of his on the very first afternoon of his summer vacation. The next six weeks were entirely his own – absolutely nothing to do. He chatted awhile, drank two cups of tea, then braced himself for the effort and said suddenly:

"Well, I think I . . ."

But the lady of the house said, "Oh, no! Mr. Jones, can't you really stay a little longer?"

Jones was always truthful. "Oh, yes," he said, "of course, I – er – can stay."

"Then please don't go."

He stayed. He drank eleven cups of tea. Night was falling. He rose again.

"Well, now," he said shyly, "I think I really . . ."

"You must go?" said the lady politely. "I thought perhaps you could have stayed to dinner. . . ."

"Oh, well, so I could, you know," Jones said, "if . . ."

"Then please stay, I'm sure my husband will be delighted."

"All right," he said feebly, "I'll stay," and he sank back into his chair, just full of tea, and miserable.

Papa came home. They had dinner. All through the meal Jones sat planning to leave at eight-thirty. All the family wondered whether Mr. Jones was stupid and sulky, or only stupid.

After dinner mamma undertook to "draw him out," and showed him photographs. She showed him all the family museum, several gross of them – photos of papa's uncle and his wife, and mamma's brother and his little boy, an awfully interesting photo of papa's uncle's friend in his Bengal uniform, an awfully well-taken photo of papa's grandfather's partner's dog, and an awfully wicked one of papa as the devil for a fancy-dress ball.

At eight-thirty Jones had examined seventy-one photographs. There were about sixty-nine more that he hadn't. Jones rose.

"I must say good night now," he pleaded.

"Say good night!" they said, "why, it's only half-past eight! Have you anything to do?"

"Nothing," he admitted, and muttered something about staying six weeks, and then laughed miserably.

Just then it turned out that the favourite child of the family, such a dear little romp, had hidden Mr. Jones's hat; so papa said that he must stay, and invited him to a pipe and a chat. Papa had the pipe and gave Jones the chat, and still he stayed. Every moment he meant to take the plunge, but couldn't. Then papa began to get very tired of Jones, and fidgeted and finally said with jocular irony, that Jones had better stay all night, they could give him a shake-down. Jones mistook his meaning and thanked him with tears in his eyes, and papa put Jones to bed in the spare room and cursed him heartily.

After breakfast next day, papa went off to his work in the City, and left Jones playing with the baby, broken-hearted. His nerve was utterly gone. He was meaning to leave all day, but the thing had got on his mind and he simply couldn't. When papa came home in the evening he was surprised and chagrined to find Jones still there. He thought to jockey him out with a jest, and said he thought he'd have to charge him for his board, he! he! The unhappy young man stared wildly for a moment, then wrung papa's hand, paid him a month's board in advance, and broke down and sobbed like a child.

In the days that followed he was moody and unapproachable. He lived, of course, entirely in the drawing-room, and the lack of air and exercise began to tell sadly on his health. He passed his time in drinking tea and looking at the photographs. He would stand for hours gazing at the photographs of papa's uncle's friend in his Bengal uniform – talking to it, sometimes swearing bitterly at it. His mind was visibly failing.

At length the crash came. They carried him upstairs in a raging delirium of fever. The illness that followed was terrible. He recognised no one, not even papa's uncle's friend in his Bengal uniform. At times he would start up from his bed and shriek, "Well, I think I . . ." and then fall back upon the pillows with a horrible laugh. Then, again, he would leap up and cry, "Another cup of tea and more photographs! More photographs! Har! Har!"

At length, after a month of agony, on the last day of his vacation, he passed away. They say that when the last moment came, he sat up in bed with a beautiful smile of confidence playing upon his face, and said, "Well – the angels are calling me; I'm afraid I really must go now. Good afternoon."

And the rushing of his spirit from its prison-house was as rapid as a hunted cat passing over a garden fence.

(1896)

Gertrude the Governess:

or, Simple Seventeen

Synopsis of Previous Chapters:
There are no Previous Chapters.

IT WAS A wild and stormy night on the West Coast of Scotland. This, however, is immaterial to the present story, as the scene is not laid in the West of Scotland. For the matter of that the weather was just as bad on the East Coast of Ireland.

But the scene of this narrative is laid in the South of England and takes place in and around Knotacentinum Towers (pronounced as if written Nosham Taws), the seat of Lord Knotacent (pronounced as if written Nosh).

But it is not necessary to pronounce either of these names in reading them.

Nosham Taws was a typical English home. The main part of the house was an Elizabethan structure of warm red brick, while the elder portion, of which the Earl was inordinately proud, still showed the outlines of a Norman Keep, to which had been added a Lancastrian Jail and a Plantagenet Orphan Asylum. From the house in all directions stretched magnificent woodland and park with oaks and elms of immemorial antiquity, while nearer the house stood raspberry bushes and geranium plants which had been set out by the Crusaders.

About the grand old mansion the air was loud with the chirping of thrushes, the cawing of partridges and the clear sweet note of the rook, while deer, antelope and other quadrupeds strutted about the lawn so tame as to eat off the sun-dial. In fact, the place was a regular menagerie.

From the house downwards through the park stretched a beautiful broad avenue laid out by Henry VII.

Lord Nosh stood upon the hearthrug of the library. Trained diplomat and statesman as he was, his stern aristocratic face was upside down with fury.

"Boy," he said, "you shall marry this girl or I disinherit you. You are no son of mine."

Young Lord Ronald, erect before him, flung back a glance as defiant as his own.

"I defy you," he said. "Henceforth you are no father of mine. I will get another. I will marry none but a woman I can love. This girl that we have never seen —"

"Fool," said the Earl, "would you throw aside our estate and name of a thousand years? The girl, I am told, is beautiful; her aunt is willing; they are French; pah! they understand such things in France."

"But your reason —"

"I give no reason," said the Earl. "Listen, Ronald, I give one month. For that time you remain here. If at the end of it you refuse me, I cut you off with a shilling."

Lord Ronald said nothing; he flung himself from the room, flung himself upon his horse and rode madly off in all directions.

As the door of the library closed upon Ronald the Earl sank into a chair. His face changed. It was no longer that of the haughty nobleman, but of the hunted criminal. "He must marry the girl," he muttered. "Soon she will know all. Tutchemoff has escaped from Siberia. He knows and will tell. The whole of the mines pass to her, this property with it, and I – but enough." He rose, walked to the sideboard, drained a dipper full of gin and bitters, and became again a high-bred English gentleman.

It was at this moment that a high dogcart, driven by a groom in the livery of Earl Nosh, might have been seen entering the avenue of Nosham Taws. Beside him sat a young girl, scarce more than a child, in fact not nearly so big as the groom.

The apple-pie hat which she wore, surmounted with black willow plumes, concealed from view a face so face-like in its appearance as to be positively facial.

It was – need we say it – Gertrude the Governess, who was this day to enter upon her duties at Nosham Taws.

At the same time that the dogcart entered the avenue at one end there might have been seen riding down it from the other a tall young man, whose long, aristocratic face proclaimed his birth and who was mounted upon a horse with a face even longer than his own.

And who is this tall young man who draws nearer to Gertrude with every revolution of the horse? Ah, who, indeed? Ah, who, who? I wonder if any of my readers could guess that this was none other than Lord Ronald.

The two were destined to meet. Nearer and nearer they came. And then still nearer. Then for one brief moment they met. As they passed Gertrude raised her head and directed towards the young nobleman two eyes so eye-like in their expression as to be absolutely circular, while Lord Ronald directed towards the occupant of the dogcart a gaze so gaze-like that nothing but a gazelle, or a gas-pipe, could have emulated its intensity.

Was this the dawn of love? Wait and see. Do not spoil the story.

Let us speak of Gertrude. Gertrude DeMongmorenci McFiggin had known neither father nor mother. They had both died years before she was born. Of her mother she knew nothing, save that she was French, was extremely beautiful, and that all her ancestors and even her business acquaintances had perished in the Revolution.)

Yet Gertrude cherished the memory of her parents. On her breast the girl wore a locket in which was enshrined a miniature of her mother, while down her neck inside at the back hung a daguerreotype of her father. She carried a portrait of her grandmother up her sleeve and had pictures of her cousins tucked inside her boot, while beneath her – but enough, quite enough.

Of her father Gertrude knew even less. That he was a highborn English gentleman who had lived as a wanderer in many lands, this was all she knew. His only legacy to Gertrude had been a Russian grammar, a Roumanian phrase-book, a theodolite, and a work on mining engineering.

From her earliest infancy Gertrude had been brought up by her aunt. Her aunt had carefully instructed her in Christian principles. She had also taught her Mohammedanism to make sure.

When Gertrude was seventeen her aunt had died of hydrophobia.

The circumstances were mysterious. There had called upon her that day a strange bearded man in the costume of the Russians. After he had left, Gertrude had found her aunt in a syncope from which she passed into an apostrophe and never recovered.

To avoid scandal it was called hydrophobia. Gertrude was thus thrown upon the world. What to do? That was the problem that confronted her.

It was while musing one day upon her fate that Gertrude's eye was struck with an advertisement.

"Wanted a governess; must possess a knowledge of French, Italian, Russian, and Roumanian, Music, and Mining Engineering. Salary, £1, 4 shillings and 4 pence halfpenny per annum. Apply between half-past eleven and twenty-five minutes to twelve at No. 41 A Decimal Six, Belgravia Terrace. The Countess of Nosh."

Gertrude was a girl of great natural quickness of apprehension, and she had not pondered over this announcement more than half an hour before she was struck with the extraordinary coincidence between the list of items desired and the things that she herself knew.

She duly presented herself at Belgravia Terrace before the Countess, who advanced to meet her with a charm which at once placed the girl at her ease.

"You are proficient in French," she asked.

"*Oh, oui,*" said Gertrude modestly.

"And Italian," continued the Countess.

"*Oh, si,*" said Gertrude.

"And German," said the Countess in delight.

"*Ah, ja,*" said Gertrude.

"And Russian?"

"*Yaw.*"

"And Roumanian?"

"*Jep.*"

Amazed at the girl's extraordinary proficiency in modern languages, the Countess looked at her narrowly. Where had she seen those lineaments before? She passed her hand over her brow in thought, and spit upon the floor, but no, the face baffled her.

"Enough," she said, "I engage you on the spot; to-morrow you go down to Nosham Taws and begin teaching the children. I must add that in addition you will be expected to aid the Earl with his Russian correspondence. He has large mining interests at Tschminsk."

Tschminsk! why did the simple word reverberate upon Gertrude's ears? Why? Because it was the name written in her father's hand on the title page of his book on mining. What mystery was here?

It was on the following day that Gertrude had driven up the avenue.

She descended from the dogcart, passed through a phalanx of liveried servants drawn up seven-deep, to each of whom she gave a sovereign as she passed and entered Nosham Taws.

"Welcome," said the Countess, as she aided Gertrude to carry her trunk upstairs.

The girl presently descended and was ushered into the library, where she was presented to the Earl. As soon as the Earl's eye fell upon the face of the new governess he started visibly. Where had he seen those lineaments? Where was it? At the races, or the theatre – on a bus – no. Some subtler thread of memory was stirring in his mind. He strode hastily to the sideboard, drained a dipper and a half of brandy, and became again the perfect English gentleman.

While Gertrude has gone to the nursery to make the acquaintance of the two tiny golden-haired children who are to be her charges, let us say something here of the Earl and his son.

Lord Nosh was the perfect type of the English nobleman and statesman. The years that he had spent in the diplomatic service at Constantinople, St. Petersburg, and Salt Lake City had given to him a peculiar finesse and noblesse, while his long residence at St. Helena, Pitcairn Island, and Hamilton, Ontario, had rendered him impervious to external impressions. As deputy-paymaster of the militia of the county he had seen something of the sterner side of military life, while his hereditary office of Groom of the Sunday Breeches had brought him into direct contact with Royalty itself.

His passion for outdoor sports endeared him to his tenants. A keen sportsman, he excelled in fox-hunting, dog-hunting, pig-killing, bat-catching and the pastimes of his class.

In this latter respect Lord Ronald took after his father.

From the start the lad had shown the greatest promise. At Eton he had made a splendid showing at battledore and shuttle-cock, and at Cambridge had been first in his class at needle-work. Already his name was whispered in connection with the All England ping-pong championship, a triumph which would undoubtedly carry with it a seat in Parliament.

Thus was Gertrude the Governess installed at Nosham Taws.

The days and the weeks sped past.

The simple charm of the beautiful orphan girl attracted all hearts. Her two little pupils became her slaves. "Me loves oo," little Rasehellfrida would say, leaning her golden head in Gertrude's lap. Even the servants loved her. The head gardener would bring a bouquet of beautiful roses to her room before she was up, the second gardener a bunch of early cauliflowers, the third a spray of late asparagus, and even the tenth and eleventh a sprig of mangel-wurzel or an armful of hay. Her room was full of gardeners all the time, while at evening the aged butler, touched at the friendless girl's loneliness, would tap softly at her door to bring her a rye whisky and seltzer or a box of Pittsburg Stogies. Even the dumb creatures seemed to admire her in their own dumb way. The dumb rooks settled on her shoulder and every dumb dog around the place followed her.

And Ronald! ah, Ronald! Yes, indeed! They had met. They had spoken.

"What a dull morning," Gertrude had said. "*Quel triste matin! Was fur ein allerverdamnter Tag!*"

"Beastly," Ronald had answered.

"Beastly!!" The word rang in Gertrude's ears all day.

After that they were constantly together. They played ten-nis and ping-pong in the day, and in the evening, in accor-dance with the stiff routine of the place, they sat down with the Earl and Countess to twenty-five-cent poker, and later still they sat together on the verandah and watched the moon sweeping in great circles around the horizon.

It was not long before Gertrude realized that Lord Ronald felt towards her a warmer feeling than that of mere ping-pong. At times in her presence he would fall, especially after dinner, into a fit of profound subtraction.

Once at night, when Gertrude withdrew to her chamber and before seeking her pillow, prepared to retire as a preliminary to disrobing – in other words, before going to bed, she flung wide the casement (opened the window) and perceived (saw) the face of Lord Ronald. He was sitting on a thorn bush beneath her, and his upturned face wore an expression of agonized pallor.

Meantime the days passed. Life at the Taws moved in the ordinary routine of a great English household. At 7 a gong sounded for rising, at 8 a horn blew for breakfast, at 8.30 a whistle sounded for prayers, at 1 a flag was run up at half-mast for lunch, at 4 a gun was fired for afternoon tea, at 9 a first bell sounded for dressing, at 9.15 a second bell for going on dressing, while at 9.30 a rocket was sent up to indicate that dinner was ready. At midnight dinner was over, and at 1 a.m. the tolling of a bell summoned the domestics to evening prayers.

Meanwhile the month allotted by the Earl to Lord Ronald was passing away. It was already July 15, then within a day or two it was July 17, and, almost immediately afterwards, July 18.

At times the Earl, in passing Ronald in the hall, would say sternly, "Remember, boy, your consent, or I disinherit you."

And what were the Earl's thoughts of Gertrude? Here was the one drop of bitterness in the girl's cup of happiness. For some reason that she could not divine the Earl showed signs of marked antipathy.

Once as she passed the door of the library he threw a boot-jack at her. On another occasion at lunch alone with her he struck her savagely across the face with a sausage.

It was her duty to translate to the Earl his Russian correspondence. She sought in it in vain for the mystery. One day a Russian telegram was handed to the Earl. Gertrude translated it to him aloud.

"Tutchemoff went to the woman. She is dead."

On hearing this the Earl became livid with fury, in fact this was the day that he struck her with the sausage.

Then one day while the Earl was absent on a bat hunt, Gertrude, who was turning over his correspondence, with that sweet feminine instinct of interest that rose superior to ill-treatment, suddenly found the key to the mystery.

Lord Nosh was not the rightful owner of the Taws. His distant cousin of the older line, the true heir, had died in a Russian prison to which the machinations of the Earl, while Ambassador at Tschminsk, had consigned him. The daughter of this cousin was the true owner of Nosham Taws.

The family story, save only that the documents before her withheld the name of the rightful heir, lay bare to Gertrude's eye.

Strange is the heart of woman. Did Gertrude turn from the Earl with spurning? No. Her own sad fate had taught her sympathy.

Yet still the mystery remained! Why did the Earl start perceptibly each time that he looked into her face? Sometimes he started as much as four centimetres, so that one could distinctly see him do it. On such occasions he would hastily drain a dipper of rum and vichy water and become again the correct English gentleman.

The denouement came swiftly. Gertrude never forgot it.

It was the night of the great ball at Nosham Taws. The whole neighbourhood was invited. How Gertrude's heart had beat with anticipation, and with what trepidation she had overhauled her scant wardrobe in order to appear not unworthy in Lord Ronald's eyes. Her resources were poor indeed, yet the inborn genius for dress that she inherited from her French mother stood her in good stead. She twined a single rose in her hair and contrived herself a dress out of a few old newspapers and the inside of an umbrella that would have graced a court. Round her waist she bound a single braid of bagstring, while a piece of old lace that had been her mother's was suspended to her ear by a thread.

Gertrude was the cynosure of all eyes. Floating to the strains of the music she presented a picture of bright girlish innocence that no one could see undisenraptured.

The ball was at its height. It was away up!

Ronald stood with Gertrude in the shrubbery. They looked into one another's eyes.

"Gertrude," he said, "I love you."

Simple words, and yet they thrilled every fibre in the girl's costume.

"Ronald!" she said, and cast herself about his neck.

At this moment the Earl appeared standing beside them in the moonlight. His stern face was distorted with indignation.

"So!" he said, turning to Ronald, "it appears that you have chosen!"

"I have," said Ronald with hauteur.

"You prefer to marry this penniless girl rather than the heiress I have selected for you."

Gertrude looked from father to son in amazement.

"Yes," said Ronald.

"Be it so," said the Earl, draining a dipper of gin which he carried, and resuming his calm. "Then I disinherit you. Leave this place, and never return to it."

"Come, Gertrude," said Ronald tenderly, "let us flee together."

Gertrude stood before them. The rose had fallen from her head. The lace had fallen from her ear and the bagstring had come undone from her waist. Her newspapers were crumpled beyond recognition. But dishevelled and illegible as she was, she was still mistress of herself.

"Never," she said firmly. "Ronald, you shall never make this sacrifice for me." Then to the Earl, in tones of ice, "There is a pride, sir, as great even as yours. The daughter of Metschnikoff McFiggin need crave a boon from no one."

With that she hauled from her bosom the daguerreotype of her father and pressed it to her lips.

The Earl started as if shot. "That name!" he cried, "that face! that photograph! stop!"

There! There is no need to finish; my readers have long since divined it. Gertrude was the heiress.

The lovers fell into one another's arms. The Earl's proud face relaxed. "God bless you," he said. The Countess and the guests came pouring out upon the lawn. The breaking day illuminated a scene of gay congratulations.

Gertrude and Ronald were wed. Their happiness was complete. Need we say more? Yes, only this. The Earl was killed in the hunting-field a few days after. The Countess was struck by lightning. The two children fell down a well. Thus the happiness of Gertrude and Ronald was complete.

(1911)

The Marine Excursion of
the Knights of Pythias

HALF-PAST six on a July morning! The Mariposa Belle is at the wharf, decked in flags, with steam up ready to start. Excursion day!

Half-past six on a July morning, and Lake Wissanotti lying in the sun as calm as glass. The opal colours of the morning light are shot from the surface of the water.

Out on the lake the last thin threads of the mist are clearing away like flecks of cotton wool.

The long call of the loon echoes over the lake. The air is cool and fresh. There is in it all the new life of the land of the silent pine and the moving waters. Lake Wissanotti in the morning sunlight! Don't talk to me of the Italian lakes, or the Tyrol or the Swiss Alps. Take them away. Move them somewhere else. I don't want them.

Excursion Day, at half-past six of a summer morning! With the boat all decked in flags and all the people in Mariposa on the wharf, and the band in peaked caps with big cornets tied to their bodies ready to play at any minute! I say! Don't tell me about the Carnival of Venice and the Delhi Durbar. Don't! I wouldn't look at them. I'd shut my eyes! For light and colour give me every time an excursion out of Mariposa down the lake to the Indian's Island out of sight in the morning mist. Talk of your Papal Zouaves and your Buckingham Palace

Guard! I want to see the Mariposa band in uniform and the Mariposa Knights of Pythias with their aprons and their insignia and their picnic baskets and their five-cent cigars!

Half-past six in the morning, and all the crowd on the wharf and the boat due to leave in half an hour. Notice it! – in half an hour. Already she's whistled twice (at six, and at six fifteen), and at any minute now, Christie Johnson will step into the pilot house and pull the string for the warning whistle that the boat will leave in half an hour. So keep ready. Don't think of running back to Smith's Hotel for the sandwiches. Don't be fool enough to try to go up to the Greek Store, next to Netley's, and buy fruit. You'll be left behind for sure if you do. Never mind the sandwiches and the fruit! Anyway, here comes Mr. Smith himself with a huge basket of provender that would feed a factory. There must be sandwiches in that. I think I can hear them clinking. And behind Mr. Smith is the German waiter from the caff with another basket – indubitably lager beer; and behind him, the bar-tender of the hotel, carrying nothing, as far as one can see. But of course if you know Mariposa you will understand that why he looks so nonchalant and empty-handed is because he has two bottles of rye whiskey under his linen duster. You know, I think, the peculiar walk of a man with two bottles of whiskey in the inside pockets of a linen coat. In Mariposa, you see, to bring beer to an excursion is quite in keeping with public opinion. But, whiskey, – well, one has to be a little careful.

Do I say that Mr. Smith is here? Why, everybody's here. There's Hussell the editor of the Newspacket, wearing a blue ribbon on his coat, for the Mariposa Knights of Pythias are, by their constitution, dedicated to temperance; and there's Henry Mullins, the manager of the Exchange Bank, also a Knight of Pythias, with a small flask of Pogram's Special in his hip pocket as a sort of amendment to the constitution. And there's Dean Drone, the Chaplain of the Order, with a fishing-rod (you never saw such green bass as lie among the rocks at

Indian's Island), and with a trolling line in case of maski-nonge, and a landing net in case of pickerel, and with his eldest daughter, Lilian Drone, in case of young men. There never was such a fisherman as the Rev. Rupert Drone.

Perhaps I ought to explain that when I speak of the excursion as being of the Knights of Pythias, the thing must not be understood in any narrow sense. In Mariposa practically everybody belongs to the Knights of Pythias just as they do to everything else. That's the great thing about the town and that's what makes it so different from the city. Everybody is in everything.

You should see them on the seventeenth of March, for example, when everybody wears a green ribbon and they're all laughing and glad, – you know what the Celtic nature is, – and talking about Home Rule.

On St. Andrew's Day every man in town wears a thistle and shakes hands with everybody else, and you see the fine old Scotch honesty beaming out of their eyes.

And on St. George's Day! – well, there's no heartiness like the good old English spirit, after all; why shouldn't a man feel glad that he's an Englishman?

Then on the Fourth of July there are stars and stripes flying over half the stores in town, and suddenly all the men are seen to smoke cigars, and to know all about Roosevelt and Bryan and the Philippine Islands. Then you learn for the first time that Jeff Thorpe's people came from Massachusetts and that his uncle fought at Bunker Hill (it must have been Bunker Hill, – anyway Jefferson will swear it was in Dakota all right enough); and you find that George Duff has a married sister in Rochester and that her husband is all right; in fact, George was down there as recently as eight years ago. Oh, it's the most American town imaginable is Mariposa, – on the fourth of July.

But wait, just wait, if you feel anxious about the solidity of the British connection, till the twelfth of the month, when everybody is wearing an orange streamer in his coat and the Orangemen (every man in town) walk in the big procession. Allegiance! Well, perhaps you remember the address they gave to the Prince of Wales on the platform of the Mariposa station as he went through on his tour to the west. I think that pretty well settled that question.

So you will easily understand that of course everybody belongs to the Knights of Pythias and the Masons and Oddfellows, just as they all belong to the Snow Shoe Club and the Girls' Friendly Society.

And meanwhile the whistle of the steamer has blown again for a quarter to seven: – loud and long this time, for any one not here now is late for certain; unless he should happen to come down in the last fifteen minutes.

What a crowd upon the wharf and how they pile on to the steamer! It's a wonder that the boat can hold them all. But that's just the marvellous thing about the Mariposa Belle.

I don't know, – I have never known, – where the steamers like the Mariposa Belle come from. Whether they are built by Harland and Wolff of Belfast, or whether, on the other hand, they are not built by Harland and Wolff of Belfast, is more than one would like to say offhand.

The Mariposa Belle always seems to me to have some of those strange properties that distinguish Mariposa itself. I mean, her size seems to vary so. If you see her there in the winter, frozen in the ice beside the wharf with a snowdrift against the windows of the pilot house, she looks a pathetic little thing the size of a butternut. But in the summer time, especially after you've been in Mariposa for a month or two, and have paddled alongside of her in a canoe, she gets larger and taller, and with a great sweep of black sides, till you see no difference between the Mariposa Belle and the Lusitania. Each one is a big steamer and that's all you can say.

Nor do her measurements help you much. She draws about eighteen inches forward, and more than that, – at least half an inch more, astern, and when she's loaded down with an excursion crowd she draws a good two inches more. And above the water, – why, look at all the decks on her! There's the deck you walk on to, from the wharf, all shut in, with windows along it, and the after cabin with the long table, and above that the deck with all the chairs piled upon it, and the deck in front where the band stand round in a circle, and the pilot house is higher than that, and above the pilot house is the board with the gold name and the flag pole and the steel ropes and the flags; and fixed in somewhere on the different levels is the lunch counter where they sell the sandwiches, and the engine room, and down below the deck level, beneath the water line, is the place where the crew sleep. What with steps and stairs and passages and piles of cordwood for the engine, – oh no, I guess Harland and Wolff didn't build her. They couldn't have.

Yet even with a huge boat like the Mariposa Belle, it would be impossible for her to carry all of the crowd that you see in the boat and on the wharf. In reality, the crowd is made up of two classes, – all of the people in Mariposa who are going on the excursion and all those who are not. Some come for the one reason and some for the other.

The two tellers of the Exchange Bank are both there standing side by side. But one of them, – the one with the cameo pin and the long face like a horse, – is going, and the other, – with the other cameo pin and the face like another horse, – is not. In the same way, Hussell of the Newspacket is going, but his brother, beside him, isn't. Lilian Drone is going, but her sister can't; and so on all through the crowd.

And to think that things should look like that on the morning of a steamboat accident.

How strange life is!

To think of all these people so eager and anxious to catch the steamer, and some of them running to catch it, and so fearful that they might miss it, – the morning of a steamboat accident. And the captain blowing his whistle, and warning them so severely that he would leave them behind, – leave them out of the accident! And everybody crowding so eagerly to be in the accident.

Perhaps life is like that all through.

Strangest of all to think, in a case like this, of the people who were left behind, or in some way or other prevented from going, and always afterwards told of how they had escaped being on board the Mariposa Belle that day!

Some of the instances were certainly extraordinary.

Nivens, the lawyer, escaped from being there merely by the fact that he was away in the city.

Towers, the tailor, only escaped owing to the fact that, not intending to go on the excursion he had stayed in bed till eight o'clock and so had not gone. He narrated afterwards that waking up that morning at half-past five, he had thought of the excursion and for some unaccountable reason had felt glad that he was not going.

The case of Yodel, the auctioneer, was even more inscrutable. He had been to the Oddfellows' excursion on the train the week before and to the Conservative picnic the week before that, and had decided not to go on this trip. In fact, he had not the least intention of going. He narrated afterwards how the night before someone had stopped him on the corner of Nippewa and Tecumseh Streets (he indicated the very spot) and asked: "Are you going to take in the excursion to-morrow?" and he had said, just as simply as he was talking when narrating it: "No." And ten minutes after that, at the corner of Dalhousie and Brock Streets (he offered to lead a party of verification to the precise place) somebody else had stopped him and asked: "Well, are you going on the steamer trip to-morrow?" Again he had answered: "No," apparently almost in the same tone as before.

He said afterwards that when he heard the rumour of the accident it seemed like the finger of Providence, and fell on his knees in thankfulness.

There was the similar case of Morison (I mean the one in Glover's hardware store that married one of the Thompsons). He said afterwards that he had read so much in the papers about accidents lately, – mining accidents, and aeroplanes and gasoline, – that he had grown nervous. The night before his wife had asked him at supper: "Are you going on the excursion?" He had answered: "No, I don't think I feel like it," and had added: "Perhaps your mother might like to go." And the next evening just at dusk, when the news ran through the town, he said the first thought that flashed through his head was: "Mrs. Thompson's on that boat."

He told this right as I say it – without the least doubt or confusion. He never for a moment imagined she was on the Lusitania or the Olympic or any other boat. He knew she was on this one. He said you could have knocked him down where he stood. But no one had. Not even when he got halfway down, – on his knees, and it would have been easier still to knock him down or kick him. People do miss a lot of chances.

Still, as I say, neither Yodel nor Morison nor anyone thought about there being an accident until just after sundown when they –

Well, have you ever heard the long booming whistle of a steamboat two miles out on the lake in the dusk, and while you listen and count and wonder, seen the crimson rockets going up against the sky and then heard the fire bell ringing right there beside you in the town, and seen the people running to the town wharf?

That's what the people of Mariposa saw and felt that summer evening as they watched the Mackinaw life-boat go plunging out into the lake with seven sweeps to a side and the foam clear to the gunwale with the lifting stroke of fourteen men!

But, dear me, I am afraid that this is no way to tell a story. I suppose the true art would have been to have said nothing about the accident till it happened. But when you write about Mariposa, or hear of it, if you know the place, it's all so vivid and real that a thing like the contrast between the excursion crowd in the morning and the scene at night leaps into your mind and you must think of it.

But never mind about the accident, – let us turn back again to the morning.

The boat was due to leave at seven. There was no doubt about the hour, – not only seven, but seven sharp. The notice in the Newspacket said: "The boat will leave sharp at seven;" and the advertising posters on the telegraph poles on Missinaba Street that began "Ho, for Indian's Island!" ended up with the words: "Boat leaves at seven sharp." There was a big notice on the wharf that said: "Boat leaves sharp on time."

So at seven, right on the hour, the whistle blew loud and long, and then at seven fifteen three short peremptory blasts, and at seven thirty one quick angry call, – just one, – and very soon after that they cast off the last of the ropes and the Mariposa Belle sailed off in her cloud of flags, and the band of the Knights of Pythias, timing it to a nicety, broke into the "Maple Leaf for Ever!"

I suppose that all excursions when they start are much the same. Anyway, on the Mariposa Belle everybody went running up and down all over the boat with deck chairs and camp stools and baskets, and found places, splendid places to sit, and then got scared that there might be better ones and chased off again. People hunted for places out of the sun and when they got them swore that they weren't going to freeze to please anybody; and the people in the sun said that they hadn't paid fifty cents to be roasted. Others said that they hadn't paid fifty cents to get covered with cinders, and there were still others who hadn't paid fifty cents to get shaken to death with the propeller.

Still, it was all right presently. The people seemed to get sorted out into the places on the boat where they belonged. The women, the older ones, all gravitated into the cabin on the lower deck and by getting round the table with needlework, and with all the windows shut, they soon had it, as they said themselves, just like being at home.

All the young boys and the toughs and the men in the band got down on the lower deck forward, where the boat was dirtiest and where the anchor was and the coils of rope.

And upstairs on the after deck there were Lilian Drone and Miss Lawson, the high school teacher, with a book of German poetry, – Gothey I think it was, – and the bank teller and the younger men.

In the centre, standing beside the rail, were Dean Drone and Dr. Gallagher, looking through binocular glasses at the shore.

Up in front on the little deck forward of the pilot house was a group of the older men, Mullins and Duff and Mr. Smith in a deck chair, and beside him Mr. Golgotha Gingham, the undertaker of Mariposa, on a stool. It was part of Mr. Gingham's principles to take in an outing of this sort, a business matter, more or less, – for you never know what may happen at these water parties. At any rate, he was there in a neat suit of black, not, of course, his heavier or professional suit, but a soft clinging effect as of burnt paper that combined gaiety and decorum to a nicety.

"Yes," said Mr. Gingham, waving his black glove in a general way towards the shore, "I know the lake well, very well. I've been pretty much all over it in my time."

"Canoeing?" asked somebody.

"No," said Mr. Gingham, "not in a canoe." There seemed a peculiar and quiet meaning in his tone.

"Sailing, I suppose," said somebody else.

"No," said Mr. Gingham. "I don't understand it."

"I never knowed that you went on to the water at all, Gol," said Mr. Smith, breaking in.

"Ah, not now," explained Mr. Gingham; "it was years ago, the first summer I came to Mariposa. I was on the water practically all day. Nothing like it to give a man an appetite and keep him in shape."

"Was you camping?" asked Mr. Smith.

"We camped at night," assented the undertaker, "but we put in practically the whole day on the water. You see we were after a party that had come up here from the city on his vacation and gone out in a sailing canoe. We were dragging. We were up every morning at sunrise, lit a fire on the beach and cooked breakfast, and then we'd light our pipes and be off with the net for a whole day. It's a great life," concluded Mr. Gingham wistfully.

"Did you get him?" asked two or three together.

There was a pause before Mr. Gingham answered.

"We did," he said, – "down in the reeds past Horseshoe Point. But it was no use. He turned blue on me right away."

After which Mr. Gingham fell into such a deep reverie that the boat had steamed another half-mile down the lake before anybody broke the silence again.

Talk of this sort, – and after all what more suitable for a day on the water? – beguiled the way.

Down the lake, mile by mile over the calm water, steamed the Mariposa Belle. They passed Poplar Point where the high sand-banks are with all the swallows' nests in them, and Dean Drone and Dr. Gallagher looked at them alternately through the binocular glasses, and it was wonderful how plainly one could see the swallows and the banks and the shrubs, – just as plainly as with the naked eye.

And a little further down they passed the Shingle Beach, and Dr. Gallagher, who knew Canadian history, said to Dean Drone that it was strange to think that Champlain had landed there with his French explorers three hundred years ago; and Dean Drone, who didn't know Canadian history, said it was stranger still to think that the hand of the Almighty had piled up the hills and rocks long before that; and Dr. Gallagher said it was wonderful how the French had found their way through such a pathless wilderness; and Dean Drone said that it was wonderful also to think that the Almighty had placed even the smallest shrub in its appointed place. Dr. Gallagher said it filled him with admiration. Dean Drone said it filled him with awe. Dr. Gallagher said he'd been full of it ever since he was a boy; and Dean Drone said so had he.

Then a little further, as the Mariposa Belle steamed on down the lake, they passed the Old Indian Portage where the great grey rocks are; and Dr. Gallagher drew Dean Drone's attention to the place where the narrow canoe track wound up from the shore to the woods, and Dean Drone said he could see it perfectly well without the glasses.

Dr. Gallagher said that it was just here that a party of five hundred French had made their way with all their baggage and accoutrements across the rocks of the divide and down to the Great Bay. And Dean Drone said that it reminded him of Xenophon leading his ten thousand Greeks over the hill passes of Armenia down to the sea. Dr. Gallagher said that he had often wished he could have seen and spoken to Champlain, and Dean Drone said how much he regretted to have never known Xenophon.

And then after that they fell to talking of relics and traces of the past, and Dr. Gallagher said that if Dean Drone would come round to his house some night he would show him some Indian arrow heads that he had dug up in his garden. And Dean Drone said that if Dr. Gallagher would come round to the rectory any afternoon he would show him a map of Xerxes' invasion of Greece. Only he must come some time between the Infant Class and the Mothers' Auxiliary.

So presently they both knew that they were blocked out of one another's houses for some time to come, and Dr. Gallagher walked forward and told Mr. Smith, who had never studied Greek, about Champlain crossing the rock divide.

Mr. Smith turned his head and looked at the divide for half a second and then said he had crossed a worse one up north back of the Wahnipitae and that the flies were Hades, – and then went on playing freezeout poker with the two juniors in Duff's bank.

So Dr. Gallagher realized that that's always the way when you try to tell people things, and that as far as gratitude and appreciation goes one might as well never read books or travel anywhere or do anything.

In fact, it was at this very moment that he made up his mind to give the arrows to the Mariposa Mechanics' Institute, – they afterwards became, as you know, the Gallagher Collection. But, for the time being, the doctor was sick of them and wandered off round the boat and watched Henry Mullins showing George Duff how to make a John Collins without lemons, and finally went and sat down among the Mariposa band and wished that he hadn't come.

So the boat steamed on and the sun rose higher and higher, and the freshness of the morning changed into the full glare of noon, and they went on to where the lake began to narrow in at its foot, just where the Indian's Island is, – all grass and trees and with a log wharf running into the water. Below it the Lower Ossawippi runs out of the lake, and quite near are the rapids, and you can see down among the trees the red brick of the power house and hear the roar of the leaping water.

The Indian's Island itself is all covered with trees and tangled vines, and the water about it is so still that it's all reflected double and looks the same either way up. Then when the steamer's whistle blows as it comes into the wharf, you hear it echo among the trees of the island, and reverberate back from the shores of the lake.

The scene is all so quiet and still and unbroken, that Miss Cleghorn, – the sallow girl in the telephone exchange, that I spoke of – said she'd like to be buried there. But all the people were so busy getting their baskets and gathering up their things that no one had time to attend to it.

I mustn't even try to describe the landing and the boat crunching against the wooden wharf and all the people running to the same side of the deck and Christie Johnson calling out to the crowd to keep to the starboard and nobody being able to find it. Everyone who has been on a Mariposa excursion knows all about that.

Nor can I describe the day itself and the picnic under the trees. There were speeches afterwards, and Judge Pepperleigh gave such offence by bringing in Conservative politics that a man called Patriotus Canadiensis wrote and asked for some of the invaluable space of the Mariposa Times-Herald and exposed it.

I should say that there were races too, on the grass on the open side of the island, graded mostly according to ages, – races for boys under thirteen and girls over nineteen and all that sort of thing. Sports are generally conducted on that plan in Mariposa. It is realized that a woman of sixty has an unfair advantage over a mere child.

Dean Drone managed the races and decided the ages and gave out the prizes; the Wesleyan minister helped, and he and the young student, who was relieving in the Presbyterian Church, held the string at the winning point.

They had to get mostly clergymen for the races because all the men had wandered off, somehow, to where they were drinking lager beer out of two kegs stuck on pine logs among the trees.

But if you've ever been on a Mariposa excursion you know all about these details anyway.

So the day wore on and presently the sun came through the trees on a slant and the steamer whistle blew with a great puff of white steam and all the people came straggling down to the wharf and pretty soon the Mariposa Belle had floated out on to the lake again and headed for the town, twenty miles away.

I suppose you have often noticed the contrast there is between an excursion on its way out in the morning and what it looks like on the way home.

In the morning everybody is so restless and animated and moves to and fro all over the boat and asks questions. But coming home, as the afternoon gets later and the sun sinks beyond the hills, all the people seem to get so still and quiet and drowsy.

So it was with the people on the Mariposa Belle. They sat there on the benches and the deck chairs in little clusters, and listened to the regular beat of the propeller and almost dozed off asleep as they sat. Then when the sun set and the dusk drew on, it grew almost dark on the deck and so still that you could hardly tell there was anyone on board.

And if you had looked at the steamer from the shore or from one of the islands, you'd have seen the row of lights from the cabin windows shining on the water and the red glare of the burning hemlock from the funnel, and you'd have heard the soft thud of the propeller miles away over the lake.

Now and then, too, you could have heard them singing on

the steamer, – the voices of the girls and the men blended into unison by the distance, rising and falling in long-drawn melody: "*O – Can-a-da – O – Can-a-da.*"

You may talk as you will about the intoning choirs of your European cathedrals, but the sound of "O Can-a-da," borne across the waters of a silent lake at evening is good enough for those of us who know Mariposa.

I think that it was just as they were singing like this: "*O – Can-a-da,*" that word went round that the boat was sinking.

If you have ever been in any sudden emergency on the water, you will understand the strange psychology of it, – the way in which what is happening seems to become known all in a moment without a word being said. The news is transmitted from one to the other by some mysterious process.

At any rate, on the Mariposa Belle first one and then the other heard that the steamer was sinking. As far as I could ever learn the first of it was that George Duff, the bank manager, came very quietly to Dr. Gallagher and asked him if he thought that the boat was sinking. The doctor said no, that he had thought so earlier in the day but that he didn't now think that she was.

After that Duff, according to his own account, had said to Macartney, the lawyer, that the boat was sinking, and Macartney said that he doubted it very much.

Then somebody came to Judge Pepperleigh and woke him up and said that there was six inches of water in the steamer and that she was sinking. And Pepperleigh said it was perfect scandal and passed the news on to his wife and she said that they had no business to allow it and that if the steamer sank that was the last excursion she'd go on.

So the news went all round the boat and everywhere the people gathered in groups and talked about it in the angry and excited way that people have when a steamer is sinking on one of the lakes like Lake Wissanotti.

Dean Drone, of course, and some others were quieter

about it, and said that one must make allowances and that naturally there were two sides to everything. But most of them wouldn't listen to reason at all. I think, perhaps, that some of them were frightened. You see the last time but one that the steamer had sunk, there had been a man drowned and it made them nervous.

What? Hadn't I explained about the depth of Lake Wissanotti? I had taken it for granted that you knew; and in any case parts of it are deep enough, though I don't suppose in this stretch of it from the big reed beds up to within a mile of the town wharf, you could find six feet of water in it if you tried. Oh, pshaw! I was not talking about a steamer sinking in the ocean and carrying down its screaming crowds of people into the hideous depths of green water. Oh, dear me no! That kind of thing never happens on Lake Wissanotti.

But what does happen is that the Mariposa Belle sinks every now and then, and sticks there on the bottom till they get things straightened up.

On the lakes round Mariposa, if a person arrives late anywhere and explains that the steamer sank, everybody understands the situation.

You see when Harland and Wolff built the Mariposa Belle, they left some cracks in between the timbers that you fill up with cotton waste every Sunday. If this is not attended to, the boat sinks. In fact, it is part of the law of the province that all the steamers like the Mariposa Belle must be properly corked, – I think that is the word, – every season. There are inspectors who visit all the hotels in the province to see that it is done.

So you can imagine now that I've explained it a little straighter, the indignation of the people when they knew that the boat had come uncorked and that they might be stuck out there on a shoal or a mud-bank half the night.

I don't say either that there wasn't any danger; anyway, it doesn't feel very safe when you realize that the boat is settling down with every hundred yards that she goes, and you look over the side and see only the black water in the gathering night.

Safe! I'm not sure now that I come to think of it that it isn't worse than sinking in the Atlantic. After all, in the Atlantic there is wireless telegraphy, and a lot of trained sailors and stewards. But out on Lake Wissanotti, – far out, so that you can only just see the lights of the town away off to the south, – when the propeller comes to a stop, – and you can hear the hiss of steam as they start to rake out the engine fires to prevent an explosion, – and when you turn from the red glare that comes from the furnace doors as they open them, to the black dark that is gathering over the lake, – and there's a night wind beginning to run among the rushes, – and you see the men going forward to the roof of the pilot house to send up the rockets to rouse the town, – safe? Safe yourself, if you like; as for me, let me once get back into Mariposa again, under the night shadow of the maple trees, and this shall be the last, last time I'll go on Lake Wissanotti.

Safe! Oh yes! Isn't it strange how safe other people's adventures seem after they happen? But you'd have been scared, too, if you'd been there just before the steamer sank, and seen them bringing up all the women on to the top deck.

I don't see how some of the people took it so calmly; how Mr. Smith, for instance, could have gone on smoking and telling how he'd had a steamer "sink on him" on Lake Nipissing and a still bigger one, a side-wheeler, sink on him in Lake Abbitibbi.

Then, quite suddenly, with a quiver, down she went. You could feel the boat sink, sink, – down, down, – would it never get to the bottom? The water came flush up to the lower deck, and then, – thank heaven, – the sinking stopped and there was the Mariposa Belle safe and tight on a reed bank.

Really, it made one positively laugh! It seemed so queer and, anyway, if a man has a sort of natural courage, danger makes him laugh. Danger! pshaw! fiddlesticks! everybody scouted the idea. Why, it is just the little things like this that give zest to a day on the water.

Within half a minute they were all running round looking for sandwiches and cracking jokes and talking of making coffee over the remains of the engine fires.

I don't need to tell at length how it all happened after that.

I suppose the people on the Mariposa Belle would have had to settle down there all night or till help came from the town, but some of the men who had gone forward and were peering out into the dark said that it couldn't be more than a mile across the water to Miller's Point. You could almost see it over there to the left, – some of them, I think, said "off on the port bow," because you know when you get mixed up in these marine disasters, you soon catch the atmosphere of the thing.

So pretty soon they had the davits swung out over the side and were lowering the old lifeboat from the top deck into the water.

There were men leaning out over the rail of the Mariposa Belle with lanterns that threw the light as they let her down, and the glare fell on the water and the reeds. But when they got the boat lowered, it looked such a frail, clumsy thing as one saw it from the rail above, that the cry was raised: "Women and children first!" For what was the sense, if it should turn out that the boat wouldn't even hold women and children, of trying to jam a lot of heavy men into it?

So they put in mostly women and children and the boat pushed out into the darkness so freighted down it would hardly float.

In the bow of it was the Presbyterian student who was relieving the minister, and he called out that they were in the hands of Providence. But he was crouched and ready to spring out of them at the first moment.

So the boat went and was lost in the darkness except for the lantern in the bow that you could see bobbing on the water. Then presently it came back and they sent another load, till pretty soon the decks began to thin out and everybody got impatient to be gone.

It was about the time that the third boat-load put off that Mr. Smith took a bet with Mullins for twenty-five dollars, that he'd be home in Mariposa before the people in the boats had walked round the shore.

No one knew just what he meant, but pretty soon they saw Mr. Smith disappear down below into the lowest part of the steamer with a mallet in one hand and a big bundle of marline in the other.

They might have wondered more about it, but it was just at this time that they heard the shouts from the rescue boat – the big Mackinaw lifeboat – that had put out from the town with fourteen men at the sweeps when they saw the first rockets go up.

I suppose there is always something inspiring about a rescue at sea, or on the water.

After all, the bravery of the lifeboat man is the true bravery, – expended to save life, not to destroy it.

Certainly they told for months after of how the rescue boat came out to the Mariposa Belle.

I suppose that when they put her in the water the lifeboat touched it for the first time since the old Macdonald Government placed her on Lake Wissanotti.

Anyway, the water poured in at every seam. But not for a moment, – even with two miles of water between them and the steamer, – did the rowers pause for that.

By the time they were half-way there the water was almost up to the thwarts, but they drove her on. Panting and exhausted (for mind you, if you haven't been in a fool boat like that for years, rowing takes it out of you), the rowers stuck to their task. They threw the ballast over and chucked into the water the heavy cork jackets and lifebelts that encumbered their movements. There was no thought of turning back. They were nearer to the steamer than the shore.

"Hang to it, boys," called the crowd from the steamer's deck, and hang they did.

They were almost exhausted when they got them; men leaning from the steamer threw them ropes and one by one every man was hauled aboard just as the lifeboat sank under their feet.

Saved! by Heaven, saved, by one of the smartest pieces of rescue work ever seen on the lake.

There's no use describing it; you need to see rescue work of this kind by lifeboats to understand it.

Nor were the lifeboat crew the only ones that distinguished themselves.

Boat after boat and canoe after canoe had put out from Mariposa to the help of the steamer. They got them all.

Pupkin, the other bank teller, with a face like a horse, who hadn't gone on the excursion, – as soon as he knew that the boat was signalling for help and that Miss Lawson was sending up rockets, – rushed for a row boat, grabbed an oar (two would have hampered him), and paddled madly out into the lake. He struck right out into the dark with the crazy skiff almost sinking beneath his feet. But they got him. They rescued him. They watched him, almost dead with exhaustion, make his way to the steamer, where he was hauled up with ropes. Saved! Saved!!

They might have gone on that way half the night, picking up the rescuers, only, at the very moment when the tenth load of people left for the shore, – just as suddenly and saucily as you please, up came the Mariposa Belle from the mud bottom and floated.

FLOATED?

Why, of course she did. If you take a hundred and fifty

people off a steamer that has sunk, and if you get a man as shrewd as Mr. Smith to plug the timber seams with mallet and marline, and if you turn ten bandsmen of the Mariposa band on to your hand pump on the bow of the lower decks – float? why, what else can she do?

Then, if you stuff in hemlock into the embers of the fire that you were raking out, till it hums and crackles under the boiler, it won't be long before you hear the propeller thud – thudding at the stern again, and before the long roar of the steam whistle echoes over to the town.

And so the Mariposa Belle, with all steam up again and with the long train of sparks careering from the funnel, is heading for the town.

But no Christie Johnson at the wheel in the pilot house this time.

"Smith! Get Smith!" is the cry.

Can he take her in? Well, now! Ask a man who has had steamers sink on him in half the lakes from Temiscaming to the Bay, if he can take her in? Ask a man who has run a York boat down the rapids of the Moose when the ice is moving, if he can grip the steering wheel of the Mariposa Belle? So there she steams safe and sound to the town wharf!

Look at the lights and the crowd! If only the federal census taker could count us now! Hear them calling and shouting back and forward from the deck to the shore! Listen! There is the rattle of the shore ropes as they get them ready, and there's the Mariposa band, – actually forming in a circle on the upper deck just as she docks, and the leader with his baton, – one – two – ready now, –

"O CAN-A-DA!"

(1912)

The Dentist and the Gas

"I THINK," said the dentist, stepping outside again, "I'd better give you gas."

Then he moved aside and hummed an air from a light opera while he mixed up cement:

I sat up in my shroud.

"Gas!" I said.

"Yes," he repeated, "gas, or else ether or a sulphuric anesthetic, or else beat you into insensibility with a club, or give you three thousand bolts of electricity."

These may not have been his exact words. But they convey the feeling of them very nicely.

I could see the light of primitive criminality shining behind the man's spectacles.

. And to think that this was *my* fault – the result of my own reckless neglect. I had grown so used to sitting back dozing in my shroud in the dentist's chair, listening to the twittering of the birds outside, my eyes closed in the sweet half sleep of perfect security, that the old apprehensiveness and mental agony had practically all gone.

He didn't hurt me, and I knew it.

I had grown – I know it sounds mad – almost to like him.

For a time I had kept up the appearance of being hurt every

few minutes, just as a precaution. Then even that had ceased and I had dropped into vainglorious apathy.

It was this, of course, which had infuriated the dentist. He meant to reassert his power. He knew that nothing but gas could rouse me out of my lethargy and he meant to apply it – either gas or some other powerful pain stimulant.

So as soon as he said "*gas*," my senses were alert in a moment.

"When are you going to do it?" I said in horror.

"Right now, if you like," he answered.

His eyes were glittering with what the Germans call *Blutlust*. All dentists have it.

I could see that if I took my eye off him for a moment he might spring at me, gas in hand, and throttle me.

"No, not now, I can't stay now," I said, "I have an appointment, a whole lot of appointments, urgent ones, the most urgent I ever had." I was unfastening my shroud as I spoke.

"Well, then, to-morrow," said the dentist.

"No," I said, "to-morrow is Saturday. And Saturday is a day when I simply can't take gas. If I take gas, even the least bit of gas on a Saturday, I find it's misunderstood —"

"Monday then."

"Monday, I'm afraid, won't do. It's a bad day for me – worse than I can explain."

"Tuesday?" said the dentist.

"Not Tuesday," I answered. "Tuesday is the worst day of all. On Tuesday my church society meets, and I *must* go to it."

I hadn't been near it, in reality, for three years, but suddenly I felt a longing to attend it.

"On Wednesday," I went on, speaking hurriedly and wildly, "I have another appointment, a swimming club, and on Thursday two appointments, a choral society and a funeral. On Friday I have another funeral. Saturday is market day. Sunday is washing day. Monday is drying day —"

"Hold on," said the dentist, speaking very firmly. "You come to-morrow morning: I'll write the engagement for ten o'clock."

I think it must have been hypnotism.

Before I knew it, I had said "Yes."

I went out.

On the street I met a man I knew.

"Have you ever taken gas from a dentist?" I asked.

"Oh, yes," he said; "it's nothing."

Soon after I met another man.

"Have you ever taken gas?" I asked.

"Oh, certainly," he answered, "it's nothing, nothing at all."

Altogether I asked about fifty people that day about gas, and they all said that it was absolutely nothing. When I said that I was to take it to-morrow, they showed no concern whatever. I looked in their faces for traces of anxiety. There weren't any. They all said that it wouldn't hurt me, that it was nothing.

So then I was glad because I knew that gas was nothing.

It began to seem hardly worth while to keep the appointment. Why go all the way downtown for such a mere nothing?

But I did go.

I kept the appointment.

What followed was such an absolute nothing that I shouldn't bother to relate it except for the sake of my friends.

The dentist was there with two assistants. All three had white coats on, as rigid as naval uniforms.

I forget whether they carried revolvers.

Nothing could exceed their quiet courage. Let me pay them that tribute.

I was laid out in my shroud in a long chair and tied down to it (I think I was tied down; perhaps I was fastened with nails). This part of it was a mere nothing. It simply felt like being tied down by three strong men armed with pinchers.

After that a gas tank and a pump were placed beside me and a set of rubber tubes fastened tight over my mouth and nose.

Even those who have never taken gas can realize how ridiculously simple this is.

Then they began pumping in gas. The sensation of this part of it I cannot, unfortunately, recall. It happened that just as they began to administer the gas, I fell asleep. I don't quite know why. Perhaps I was overtired. Perhaps it was the simple home charm of the surroundings, the soft drowsy hum of the gas pump, the twittering of the dentists in the trees – did I say the trees? No; of course they weren't in the trees – imagine dentists in the trees – ha! ha! Here, take off this gaspipe from my face till I laugh – really I just want to laugh – only to laugh —

Well, – that's what it felt like.

Meanwhile they were operating.

Of course I didn't *feel* it. All I felt was that someone dealt me a powerful blow in the face with a sledgehammer. After that somebody took a pickax and cracked in my jaw with it. That was all.

It was a mere nothing. I felt at the time that a man who objects to a few taps on the face with a pickax is overcritical.

I didn't happen to wake up till they had practically finished. So I really missed the whole thing.

The assistants had gone, and the dentist was mixing up cement and humming airs from light opera just like old times. It made the world seem a bright place.

I went home with no teeth. I only meant them to remove one, but I realized that they had taken them all out. Still it didn't matter.

Not long after I received my bill. I was astounded at the nerve of it! For administering gas, debtor, so much; for removing teeth, debtor, so much; – and so on.

In return I sent in my bill:

Dr. William Jaws

DEBTOR

To mental agony	$50.00
To gross lies in regard to the nothingness of gas	100.00
To putting me under gas	50.00
To having fun with me under gas	100.00
To Brilliant Ideas, occurred to me under gas and lost	100.00
Grand Total	$400.00

My bill has been contested and is in the hands of a solicitor. The matter will prove, I understand, a test case and will go to the final courts. If the judges have toothache during the trial, I shall win.

(1913)

The Love Story of Mr. Peter Spillikins

ALMOST any day, on Plutoria Avenue or thereabouts, you may see little Mr. Spillikins out walking with his four tall sons, who are practically as old as himself.

To be exact, Mr. Spillikins is twenty-four, and Bob, the oldest of the boys, must be at least twenty. Their exact ages are no longer known, because, by a dreadful accident, their mother forgot them. This was at a time when the boys were all at Mr. Wackem's Academy for Exceptional Youths in the foothills of Tennessee, and while their mother, Mrs. Everleigh, was spending the winter on the Riviera and felt that for their own sake she must not allow herself to have the boys with her.

But now, of course, since Mrs. Everleigh has remarried and become Mrs. Everleigh-Spillikins there is no need to keep them at Mr. Wackem's any longer. Mr. Spillikins is able to look after them.

Mr. Spillikins generally wears a little top hat and an English morning coat. The boys are in Eton jackets and black trousers, which, at their mother's wish, are kept just a little too short for them. This is because Mrs. Everleigh-Spillikins feels that the day will come some day – say fifteen years hence, – when the boys will no longer be children, and meantime it is so nice to feel that they are still mere boys. Bob is the eldest, but Sib the youngest is the tallest, whereas Willie the third boy is the dullest, although this has often been denied by those who claim that Gib the second boy is just a trifle duller. Thus at any rate there is a certain equality and good fellowship all round.

(Mrs. Everleigh-Spillikins is not to be seen walking with them. She is probably at the race-meet, being taken there by Captain Cormorant of the United States navy, which Mr. Spillikins considers very handsome of him. Every now and then the captain, being in the navy, is compelled to be at sea for perhaps a whole afternoon or even several days; in which case Mrs. Everleigh-Spillikins is very generally taken to the Hunt Club or the Country Club by Lieutenant Hawk, which Mr. Spillikins regards as awfully thoughtful of him. Or if Lieutenant Hawk is also out of town for the day, as he sometimes has to be, because he is in the United States army, Mrs. Everleigh-Spillikins is taken out by old Colonel Shake, who is in the State militia and who is at leisure all the time.)

During their walks on Plutoria Avenue one may hear the four boys addressing Mr. Spillikins as "father" and "dad" in deep bull-frog voices.

"Say, dad," drawls Bob, "couldn't we all go to the ball game?"

"No, say, dad," says Gib, "let's all go back to the house and play five-cent pool in the billiard-room?"

"All right, boys," says Mr. Spillikins. And a few minutes later one may see them all hustling up the steps of the Everleigh-Spillikins's mansion, quite eager at the prospect, and all talking together.

Now the whole of this daily panorama, to the eye that can read it, represents the outcome of the tangled love story of Mr. Spillikins, which culminated during the summer house-party at Castel Casteggio, the woodland retreat of Mr. and Mrs. Newberry.

But to understand the story one must turn back a year or so

to the time when Mr. Peter Spillikins used to walk on Plutoria Avenue alone, or sit in the Mausoleum Club listening to the advice of people who told him that he really ought to get married.

In those days the first thing that one noticed about Mr. Peter Spillikins was his exalted view of the other sex. Every time he passed a beautiful woman in the street he said to himself, "I say!" Even when he met a moderately beautiful one he murmured, "By Jove!" When an Easter hat went sailing past, or a group of summer parasols stood talking on a leafy corner, Mr. Spillikins ejaculated, "My word!" At the opera and at tango teas his projecting blue eyes almost popped out of his head.

Similarly, if he happened to be with one of his friends, he would murmur, "I say, *do* look at that beautiful girl," or would exclaim, "I say, don't look, but isn't that an awfully pretty girl across the street?" or at the opera, "Old man, don't let her see you looking, but do you see that lovely girl in the box opposite?"

One must add to this that Mr. Spillikins, in spite of his large and bulging blue eyes, enjoyed the heavenly gift of short sight. As a consequence he lived in a world of amazingly beautiful women. And as his mind was focussed in the same way as his eyes he endowed them with all the virtues and graces which ought to adhere to fifty-dollar flowered hats and cerise parasols with ivory handles.

Nor, to do him justice, did Mr. Spillikins confine this attitude to his view of women alone. He brought it to bear on everything. Every time he went to the opera he would come away enthusiastic, saying, "By Jove, isn't it simply splendid! Of course, I haven't the ear to appreciate it – I'm not musical, you know – but even with the little that I know, it's great; it absolutely puts me to sleep." And of each new novel that he bought he said, "It's a perfectly wonderful book! Of course I haven't the head to understand it, so I didn't finish it, but it's simply thrilling." Similarly with painting, "It's one of the most marvellous pictures I ever saw," he would say. "Of course I've no eye for pictures, and I couldn't see anything in it, but it's wonderful!"

The career of Mr. Spillikins up to the point of which we are speaking had hitherto not been very satisfactory, or at least not from the point of view of Mr. Boulder, who was his uncle and trustee. Mr. Boulder's first idea had been to have Mr. Spillikins attend the university. Dr. Boomer, the president, had done his best to spread abroad the idea that a university education was perfectly suitable even for the rich; that it didn't follow that because a man was a university graduate he need either work or pursue his studies any further; that what the university aimed to do was merely to put a certain stamp upon a man. That was all. And this stamp, according to the tenor of the president's convocation addresses, was perfectly harmless. No one ought to be afraid of it. As a result, a great many of the very best young men in the City, who had no need for education at all, were beginning to attend college. "It marked," said Dr. Boomer, "a revolution."

Mr. Spillikins himself was fascinated with his studies. The professors seemed to him living wonders.

"By Jove!" he said, "the professor of mathematics is a marvel. You ought to see him explaining trigonometry on the blackboard. You can't understand a word of it." He hardly knew which of his studies he liked best. "Physics," he said, "is a wonderful study. I got five per cent. in it. But, by Jove! I had to work for it. I'd go in for it altogether if they'd let me."

But that was just the trouble – they wouldn't. And so in course of time Mr. Spillikins was compelled, for academic reasons, to abandon his life-work. His last words about it were, "Gad! I nearly passed in trigonometry!" and he always said afterwards that he had got a tremendous lot out of the university.

After that, as he had to leave the university, his trustee, Mr.
Boulder, put Mr. Spillikins into business. It was, of course, his
own business, one of the many enterprises for which Mr. Spillikins, ever since he was twenty-one, had already been signing
documents and countersigning cheques. So Mr. Spillikins
found himself in a mahogany office selling wholesale oil.
And he liked it. He said that business sharpened one up
tremendously.

"I'm afraid, Mr. Spillikins," a caller in the mahogany office
would say, "that we can't meet you at five dollars. Four seventy
is the best we can do on the present market."

"My dear chap," said Mr. Spillikins, "that's all right. After
all, thirty cents isn't much, eh what? Dash it, old man, we
won't fight about thirty cents. How much do you want?"

"Well, at four seventy we'll take twenty thousand barrels."

"By Jove!" said Mr. Spillikins; "twenty thousand barrels.
Gad! you want a lot, don't you? Pretty big sale, eh, for a
beginner like me? I guess uncle'll be tickled to death."

So tickled was he that after a few weeks of oil selling Mr.
Boulder urged Mr. Spillikins to retire, and wrote off many
thousand dollars from the capital value of his estate.

So after this there was only one thing for Mr. Spillikins to
do, and everybody told him so – namely, to get married.

"Spillikins," said his friends at the club after they had taken
all his loose money over the card table, "you ought to get
married."

"Think so?" said Mr. Spillikins.

Goodness knows he was willing enough. In fact, up to this
point Mr. Spillikins's whole existence had been one long
aspiring sigh directed towards the joys of matrimony.

In his brief college days his timid glances had wandered by
an irresistible attraction towards the seats on the right-hand
side of the classroom, where the girls of the first year sat, with
golden pigtails down their backs, doing trigonometry.

He would have married any of them. But when a girl can

work out trigonometry at sight, what use can she possibly have for marriage? None. Mr. Spillikins knew this and it kept him silent. And even when the most beautiful girl in the class married the demonstrator and thus terminated her studies in her second year, Spillikins realised that it was only because the man was, undeniably, a demonstrator and knew things.

Later on, when Spillikins went into business and into society, the same fate pursued him. He loved, for at least six months, Georgiana McTeague, the niece of the presbyterian minister of St. Osoph's. He loved her so well that for her sake he temporarily abandoned his pew at St. Asaph's, which was episcopalian, and listened to fourteen consecutive sermons on hell. But the affair got no further than that. Once or twice indeed, Spillikins walked home with Georgiana from church and talked about hell with her; and once her uncle asked him into the manse for cold supper after evening service, and they had a long talk about hell all through the meal and upstairs in the sitting-room afterwards. But somehow Spillikins could get no further with it. He read up all he could about hell so as to be able to talk with Georgiana, but in the end it failed: a young minister fresh from college came and preached at St Osoph's six special sermons on the absolute certainty of eternal punishment, and he married Miss McTeague as a result of it.

And meantime Mr. Spillikins had got engaged, or practically so, to Adelina Lightleigh; not that he had spoken to her, but he considered himself bound to her. For her sake he had given up hell altogether, and was dancing till two in the morning and studying auction bridge out of a book. For a time he felt so sure that she meant to have him that he began bringing his greatest friend, Edward Ruff, of the college football team, of whom Spillikins was very proud, up to the Lightleighs' residence. He specially wanted Adelina and Edward to be great friends, so that Adelina and he might ask Edward up to the house after he was married. And they got to be such great friends, and so quickly, that they were married in New York that autumn. After which Spillikins used to be invited up to the house by Edward and Adelina. They both used to tell him how much they owed him; and they too used to join in the chorus and say, "You know, Peter, you're awfully silly not to get married."

Now all this had happened and finished at about the time when the Yahi-Bahi Society ran its course. At its first meeting Mr. Spillikins had met Dulphemia Rasselyer-Brown. At the very sight of her he began reading up the life of Buddha and a translation of the Upanishads so as to fit himself to aspire to live with her. Even when the society ended in disaster Mr. Spillikins's love only burned the stronger. Consequently, as soon as he knew that Mr. and Mrs. Rasselyer-Brown were going away for the summer, and that Dulphemia was to go to stay with the Newberrys at Castel Casteggio, this latter place, the summer retreat of the Newberrys, became the one spot on earth for Mr. Peter Spillikins.

Naturally, therefore, Mr. Spillikins was presently transported to the seventh heaven when in due course of time he received a note which said, "We shall be so pleased if you can come out and spend a week or two with us here. We will send the car down to the Thursday train to meet you. We live here in the simplest fashion possible; in fact, as Mr. Newberry says, we are just roughing it, but I am sure you don't mind for a change. Dulphemia is with us, but we are quite a small party."

The note was signed "Margaret Newberry" and was written on heavy cream paper with a silver monogram such as people use when roughing it.

The Newberrys, like everybody else, went away from town in the summer-time. Mr. Newberry being still in business, after a fashion, it would not have looked well for him to remain in town throughout the year. It would have created a bad impression on the market as to how much he was making.

In fact, in the early summer everybody went out of town. The few who ever revisited the place in August reported that they hadn't seen a soul on the street.

It was a sort of longing for the simple life, for nature, that came over everybody. Some people sought it at the seaside, where nature had thrown out her broad plank walks and her long piers and her vaudeville shows. Others sought it in the heart of the country, where nature had spread her oiled motor roads and her wayside inns. Others, like the Newberrys, preferred to "rough it" in country residences of their own.

Some of the people, as already said, went for business reasons, to avoid the suspicion of having to work all the year round. Others went to Europe to avoid the reproach of living always in America. Others, perhaps most people, went for medical reasons, being sent away by their doctors. Not that they were ill; but the doctors of Plutoria Avenue, such as Doctor Slyder, always preferred to send all their patients out of town during the summer months. No well-to-do doctor cares to be bothered with them. And of course patients, even when they are anxious to go anywhere on their own account, much prefer to be sent there by their doctor.

"My dear madam," Dr. Slyder would say to a lady who, as he knew, was most anxious to go to Virginia, "there's really nothing I can do for you." Here he spoke the truth. "It's not a case of treatment. It's simply a matter of dropping everything and going away. Now why don't you go for a month or two to some quiet place, where you will simply *do nothing*?" (She never, as he knew, did anything, anyway.) "What do you say to Hot Springs, Virginia? – absolute quiet, good golf, not a soul there, plenty of tennis." Or else he would say, "My dear madam, you're simply *worn out*. Why don't you just drop everything and go to Canada? – perfectly quiet, not a soul there, and, I believe, nowadays quite fashionable."

Thus, after all the patients had been sent away, Dr. Slyder and his colleagues of Plutoria Avenue managed to slip away themselves for a month or two, heading straight for Paris and Vienna. There they were able, so they said, to keep in touch with what continental doctors were doing. They probably were.

Now it so happened that both the parents of Miss Dulphemia Rasselyer-Brown had been sent out of town in this fashion. Mrs. Rasselyer-Brown's distressing experience with Yahi-Bahi had left her in a condition in which she was utterly fit for nothing, except to go on a Mediterranean cruise, with about eighty other people also fit for nothing.

Mr. Rasselyer-Brown himself, though never exactly an invalid, had confessed that after all the fuss of the Yahi-Bahi business he needed bracing up, needed putting into shape, and had put himself into Dr. Slyder's hands. The doctor had examined him, questioned him searchingly as to what he drank, and ended by prescribing port wine to be taken firmly and unflinchingly during the evening, and for the daytime, at any moment of exhaustion, a light cordial such as rye whiskey, or rum and Vichy water. In addition to which Dr. Slyder had recommended Mr. Rasselyer-Brown to leave town.

"Why don't you go down to Nagahakett on the Atlantic?" he said.

"Is that in Maine?" said Mr. Rasselyer-Brown in horror.

"Oh, dear me, no!" answered the doctor reassuringly. "It's in New Brunswick, Canada; excellent place, most liberal license laws; first class cuisine and bar in the hotel. No tourists, no golf, too cold to swim – just the place to enjoy oneself."

So Mr. Rasselyer-Brown had gone away also, and as a result Dulphemia Rasselyer-Brown, at the particular moment of which we speak, was declared by the Boudoir and Society column of the *Plutorian Daily Dollar* to be staying with Mr. and Mrs. Newberry at their charming retreat, Castel Casteggio.

The Newberrys belonged to the class of people whose one aim in the summer is to lead the simple life. Mr. Newberry himself said that his one idea of a vacation was to get right out into the bush, and put on old clothes, and just eat when he felt like it.

This was why he had built Castel Casteggio. It stood about forty miles from the city, out among the wooded hills on the shore of a little lake. Except for the fifteen or twenty residences like it that dotted the sides of the lake, it was entirely isolated. The only way to reach it was by the motor road that wound its way among leafy hills from the railway station fifteen miles away. Every foot of the road was private property, as all nature ought to be. The whole country about Castel Casteggio was absolutely primeval, or at any rate as primeval as Scotch gardeners and French landscape artists could make it. The lake itself lay like a sparkling gem from nature's workshop – except that they had raised the level of it ten feet, stone-banked the sides, cleared out the brush, and put a motor road round it. Beyond that it was pure nature.

Castel Casteggio itself, a beautiful house of white brick with sweeping piazzas and glittering conservatories, standing among great trees with rolling lawns broken with flower-beds as the ground sloped to the lake, was perhaps the most beautiful house of all; at any rate, it was an ideal spot to wear old clothes in, to dine early (at 7.30) and, except for tennis parties, motor boat parties, lawn teas, and golf, to live absolutely to oneself.

It should be explained that the house was not called Castel Casteggio because the Newberrys were Italian: they were not; nor because they owned estates in Italy: they didn't; nor had travelled there: they hadn't. Indeed, for a time they had thought of giving it a Welsh name, or a Scotch.

But the beautiful country residence of the Asterisk-Thomsons that stood close by in the same primeval country was already called Pennygw-rydd, and the woodland retreat of the Hyphen-Joneses just across the little lake was called Strathythan-na-Clee, and the charming châlet of the Wilson-Smiths was called Yodel-Dudel; so it seemed fairer to select an Italian name.

"By Jove! Miss Furlong, how awfully good of you to come down!"

The little suburban train – two cars only, both first class, for the train went nowhere except out into the primeval wilderness – had drawn up at the diminutive roadside station. Mr. Spillikins had alighted, and there was Miss Philippa Furlong sitting behind the chauffeur in the Newberrys' motor. She was looking as beautiful as only the younger sister of a High Church episcopalian rector can look, dressed in white, the colour of saintliness, on a beautiful morning in July.

There was no doubt about Philippa Furlong. Her beauty was of that peculiar and almost sacred kind found only in the immediate neighbourhood of the High Church clergy. It was admitted by all who envied or admired her that she could enter a church more gracefully, move more swimmingly up the aisle, and pray better than any girl on Plutoria Avenue.

Mr. Spillikins, as he gazed at her in her white summer dress and wide picture hat, with her parasol nodding above her head, realised that after all, religion, as embodied in the younger sisters of the High Church clergy, fills a great place in the world.

"By Jove!" he repeated, "how awfully good of you!"

"Not a bit," said Philippa. "Hop in. Dulphemia was coming, but she couldn't. Is that all you have with you?"

The last remark was ironical. It referred to the two quite large steamer trunks of Mr. Spillikins that were being loaded,

together with his suit-case, tennis racket, and golf kit, on to
the fore part of the motor. Mr. Spillikins, as a young man of
social experience, had roughed it before. He knew what a lot
of clothes one needs for it.

So the motor sped away, and went bowling noiselessly
over the oiled road, and turning corners where the green
boughs of the great trees almost swished in their faces, and
rounding and twisting among curves of the hills as it carried
Spillikins and Philippa away from the lower domain or ordinary fields and farms up into the enchanted country of
private property and the magic castles of Casteggio and
Pennygw-rydd.

Mr. Spillikins must have assured Philippa at least a dozen
times in starting off how awfully good it was of her to come
down in the motor; and he was so pleased at her coming to
meet him that Philippa never even hinted that the truth was
that she had expected somebody else on the same train. For to
a girl brought up in the principles of the High Church the
truth is a very sacred thing. She keeps it to herself.

And naturally, with such a sympathetic listener, it was not
long before Mr. Spillikins had begun to talk of Dulphemia and
his hopes.

"I don't know whether she really cares for me or not," said
Mr. Spillikins, "but I have pretty good hope. The other day,
or at least about two months ago, at one of the Yahi-Bahi
meetings – you were not in that, were you?" he said, breaking
off.

"Only just at the beginning," said Philippa; "we went to
Bermuda."

"Oh yes, I remember. Do you know, I thought it pretty
rough at the end, especially on Ram Spudd. I liked him. I sent
him two pounds of tobacco to the penitentiary last week; you
can get it in to them, you know, if you know how."

"But what were you going to say?" asked Philippa.

"Oh yes," said Mr. Spillikins. And he realised that he had

actually drifted off the topic of Dulphemia, a thing that had never happened to him before. "I was going to say that at one of the meetings, you know, I asked her if I might call her Dulphemia."

"And what did she say to that?" asked Philippa.

"She said she didn't care what I called her. So I think that looks pretty good, don't you?"

"Awfully good," said Philippa.

"And a little after that I took her slippers home from the Charity Ball at the Grand Palaver. Archie Jones took her home herself in his car, but I took her slippers. She'd forgotten them. I thought that a pretty good sign, wasn't it? You wouldn't let a chap carry round your slippers unless you knew him pretty well, would you, Miss Philippa?"

"Oh no, nobody would," said Philippa. This, of course, was a standing principle of the Anglican Church.

"And a little after that Dulphemia and Charlie Mostyn and I were walking to Mrs. Buncomhearst's musical, and we'd only just started along the street, when she stopped and sent me back for her music – me, mind you, not Charlie. That seems to me awfully significant."

"It seems to speak volumes," said Philippa.

"Doesn't it?" said Mr. Spillikins. "You don't mind my telling you all about this, Miss Philippa?" he added.

Incidentally Mr. Spillikins felt that it was all right to call her Miss Philippa, because she had a sister who was really Miss Furlong, so it would have been quite wrong, as Mr. Spillikins realised, to have called Miss Philippa by her surname. In any case, the beauty of the morning was against it.

"I don't mind a bit," said Philippa. "I think it's awfully nice of you to tell me about it."

She didn't add that she knew all about it already.

"You see," said Mr. Spillikins, "you're so awfully sympathetic. It makes it so easy to talk to you. With other girls, especially with clever ones, even with Dulphemia, I often feel a perfect jackass beside them. But I don't feel that way with you at all."

"Don't you really?" said Philippa, but the honest admiration in Mr. Spillikins's protruding blue eyes forbade a sarcastic answer.

"By Jove!" said Mr. Spillikins presently, with complete irrelevance, "I hope you don't mind my saying it, but you look awfully well in white – stunning." He felt that a man who was affianced, or practically so, was allowed the smaller liberty of paying honest compliments.

"Oh, this old thing," laughed Philippa, with a contemptuous shake of her dress. "But up here, you know, we just wear anything." She didn't say that this old thing was only two weeks old and had cost eighty dollars, or the equivalent of one person's pew rent at St. Asaph's for six months.

And after that they had only time, so it seemed to Mr. Spillikins, for two or three remarks, and he had scarcely had leisure to reflect what a charming girl Philippa had grown to be since she went to Bermuda – the effect, no doubt, of the climate of those fortunate islands – when quite suddenly they rounded a curve into an avenue of nodding trees, and there were the great lawn and wide piazzas and the conservatories of Castel Casteggio right in front of them.

"Here we are," said Philippa, "and there's Mr. Newberry out on the lawn."

"Now, here," Mr. Newberry was saying a little later, waving his hand, "is where you get what I think the finest view of the place."

He was standing at the corner of the lawn where it sloped, dotted with great trees, to the banks of the little lake, and was showing Mr. Spillikins the beauties of Castel Casteggio.

Mr. Newberry wore on his short circular person the summer costume of a man taking his ease and careless of dress:

plain white flannel trousers, not worth more than six dollars a leg, an ordinary white silk shirt with a rolled collar, that couldn't have cost more than fifteen dollars, and on his head an ordinary Panama hat, say forty dollars.

"By Jove!" said Mr. Spillikins, as he looked about him at the house and the beautiful lawn with its great trees, "it's a lovely place."

"Isn't it?" said Mr. Newberry. "But you ought to have seen it when I took hold of it. To make the motor road alone I had to dynamite out about a hundred yards of rock, and then I fetched up cement, tons and tons of it, and boulders to buttress the embankment."

"Did you really!" said Mr. Spillikins, looking at Mr. Newberry with great respect.

"Yes, and even that was nothing to the house itself. Do you know, I had to go at least forty feet for the foundations. First I went through about twenty feet of loose clay, after that I struck sand, and I'd no sooner got through that than, by George! I landed in eight feet of water. I had to pump it out; I think I took out a thousand gallons before I got clear down to the rock. Then I took my solid steel beams in fifty-foot lengths," here Mr. Newberry imitated with his arms the action of a man setting up a steel beam, "and set them upright and bolted them on the rock. After that I threw my steel girders across, clapped on my roof rafters, all steel, in sixty-foot pieces, and then just held it easily, just supported it a bit, and let it sink gradually to its place."

Mr. Newberry illustrated with his two arms the action of a huge house being allowed to sink slowly to a firm rest.

"You don't say so!" said Mr. Spillikins, lost in amazement at the wonderful physical strength that Mr. Newberry must have.

"Excuse me just a minute," broke off Mr. Newberry, "while I smooth out the gravel where you're standing. You've rather disturbed it, I'm afraid."

"Oh, I'm awfully sorry," said Mr. Spillikins.

"Oh, not at all, not at all," said his host. "I don't mind in the least. It's only on account of McAlister."

"Who?" asked Mr. Spillikins.

"My gardener. He doesn't care to have us walk on the gravel paths. It scuffs up the gravel so. But sometimes one forgets."

It should be said here, for the sake of clearness, that one of the chief glories of Castel Casteggio lay in its servants. All of them, it goes without saying, had been brought from Great Britain. The comfort they gave to Mr. and Mrs. Newberry was unspeakable. In fact, as they themselves admitted, servants of the kind are simply not to be found in America.

"Our Scotch gardener," Mrs. Newberry always explained, "is a perfect character. I don't know how we could get another like him. Do you know, my dear, he simply *won't allow* us to pick the roses; and if any of us walk across the grass he is furious. And he positively refuses to let us use the vegetables. He told me quite plainly that if we took any of his young peas or his early cucumbers he would leave. We are to have them later on when he's finished growing them."

"How delightful it is to have servants of that sort," the lady addressed would murmur; "so devoted and so different from servants on this side of the water. Just imagine, my dear, my chauffeur, when I was in Colorado, actually threatened to leave me merely because I wanted to reduce his wages. I think it's these wretched labour unions."

"I'm sure it is. Of course we have trouble with McAlister at times, but he's always very reasonable when we put things in the right light. Last week, for example, I was afraid that we had gone too far with him. He is always accustomed to have a quart of beer every morning at half-past ten – the maids are told to bring it out to him, and after that he goes to sleep in the little arbour beside the tulip bed. And the other day when he went there he found that one of our guests who hadn't been told, was actually sitting in there reading. Of course he was *furious.* I was afraid for the moment that he would give notice on the spot."

"What *would* you have done?"

"Positively, my dear, I don't know. But we explained to him at once that it was only an accident and that the person hadn't known and that of course it wouldn't occur again. After that he was softened a little, but he went off muttering to himself, and that evening he dug up all the new tulips and threw them over the fence. We saw him do it, but we didn't dare say anything."

"Oh no," echoed the other lady; "if you had you might have lost him."

"Exactly. And I don't think we could possibly get another man like him; at least, not on this side of the water."

"But come," said Mr. Newberry, after he had finished adjusting the gravel with his foot, "there are Mrs. Newberry and the girls on the verandah. Let's go and join them."

A few minutes later Mr. Spillikins was talking with Mrs. Newberry and Dulphemia Rasselyer-Brown, and telling Mrs. Newberry what a beautiful house she had. Beside them stood Philippa Furlong, and she had her arm around Dulphemia's waist; and the picture that they thus made, with their heads close together, Dulphemia's hair being golden and Philippa's chestnut-brown, was such that Mr. Spillikins had no eyes for Mrs. Newberry nor for Castel Casteggio nor for anything. So much so that he practically didn't see at all the little girl in green that stood unobtrusively on the further side of Mrs. Newberry. Indeed, though somebody had murmured her name in introduction, he couldn't have repeated it if asked two minutes afterwards. His eyes and his mind were elsewhere.

But hers were not.

For the Little Girl in Green looked at Mr. Spillikins with wide eyes, and when she looked at him she saw all at once such wonderful things about him as nobody had ever seen before.

For she could see from the poise of his head how awfully clever he was; and from the way he stood with his hands in his side pockets she could see how manly and brave he must be; and of course there was firmness and strength written all over him. In short, she saw as she looked such a Peter Spillikins as truly never existed, or could exist – or at least such a Peter Spillikins as no one else in the world had ever suspected before.

All in a moment she was ever so glad that she accepted Mrs. Newberry's invitation to Castel Casteggio and hadn't been afraid to come. For the Little Girl in Green, whose Christian name was Norah, was only what is called a poor relation of Mrs. Newberry, and her father was a person of no account whatever, who didn't belong to the Mausoleum Club or to any other club, and who lived, with Norah, on a street that nobody who was anybody lived upon. Norah had been asked up a few days before out of the City to give her air – which is the only thing that can be safely and freely given to poor relations. Thus she had arrived at Castel Casteggio with one diminutive trunk, so small and shabby that even the servants who carried it upstairs were ashamed of it. In it were a pair of brand new tennis shoes (at ninety cents reduced to seventy-five), and a white dress of the kind that is called "almost evening," and such few other things as poor relations might bring with fear and trembling to join in the simple rusticity of the rich.

Thus stood Norah looking at Mr. Spillikins.

As for him, such is the contrariety of human things, he had no eyes for her at all.

"What a perfectly charming house this is," Mr. Spillikins was saying. He always said this on such occasions, but it seemed to the Little Girl in Green that he spoke with wonderful social ease.

"I am so glad you think so," said Mrs. Newberry (this was what she always answered); "you've no idea what work it has been. This year we put in all this new glass in the east conservatory, over a thousand panes. Such a tremendous business!"

"I was just telling Mr. Spillikins," said Mr. Newberry, "about the work we had blasting out the motor road. You can see the gap where it lies better from here, I think, Spillikins. I must have exploded a ton and a half of dynamite on it."

"By Jove!" said Mr. Spillikins; "it must be dangerous work, eh? I wonder you aren't afraid of it."

"One simply gets used to it, that's all," said Newberry, shrugging his shoulders; "but of course it *is* dangerous. I blew up two Italians on the last job." He paused a minute and added musingly, "Hardy fellows, the Italians. I prefer them to any other people for the blasting."

"Did you blow them up yourself?" asked Mr. Spillikins.

"I wasn't here," answered Mr. Newberry. "In fact, I never care to be here when I'm blasting. We go to town. But I had to foot the bill for them all the same. Quite right, too. The risk, of course, was mine, not theirs; that's the law, you know. They cost me two thousand each."

"But come," said Mrs. Newberry, "I think we must go and dress for dinner. Franklin will be frightfully put out if we're late. Franklin is our butler," she went on, seeing that Mr. Spillikins didn't understand the reference, "and as we brought him out from England we have to be rather careful. With a good man like Franklin one is always so afraid of losing him – and after last night we have to be doubly careful."

"Why last night?" asked Mr. Spillikins.

"Oh, it wasn't much," said Mrs. Newberry. "In fact, it was merely an accident. Only it just chanced that at dinner, quite late in the meal, when we had had nearly everything (we dine very simply here, Mr. Spillikins), Mr. Newberry, who was thirsty and who wasn't really thinking what he was saying, asked Franklin to give him a glass of hock. Franklin said at once, 'I'm very sorry, sir, I don't care to serve my hock after the entrée!'"

"And of course he was right," said Dulphemia with emphasis.

"Exactly; he was perfectly right. They know, you know. We were afraid that there might be trouble, but Mr. Newberry went and saw Franklin afterwards and he behaved very well over it. But suppose we go and dress? It's half-past six already and we've only an hour."

In this congenial company Mr. Spillikins spent the next three days.

Life at Castel Casteggio, as the Newberrys loved to explain, was conducted on the very simplest plan. Early breakfast, country fashion, at nine o'clock; after that nothing to eat till lunch, unless one cared to have lemonade or bottled ale sent out with a biscuit or a macaroon to the tennis court. Lunch itself was a perfectly plain midday meal, lasting till about 1.30, and consisting simply of cold meats (say four kinds) and salads, with perhaps a made dish or two, and, for anybody who cared for it, a hot steak or a chop, or both. After that one had coffee and cigarettes in the shade of the piazza and waited for afternoon tea. This latter was served at a wicker table in any part of the grounds that the gardener was not at that moment clipping, trimming, or otherwise using. Afternoon tea being over, one rested or walked on the lawn till it was time to dress for dinner.

This simple routine was broken only by irruptions of people in motors or motor boats from Pennygw-rydd or Yodel-Dudel Châlet.

The whole thing, from the point of view of Mr. Spillikins or Dulphemia or Philippa, represented rusticity itself.

To the Little Girl in Green it seemed as brilliant as the Court of Versailles; especially evening dinner – a plain home meal as the others thought it – when she had four glasses to drink out of and used to wonder over such problems as whether you were supposed, when Franklin poured out wine, to tell him to stop or to wait till he stopped without being told to stop; and other similar mysteries, such as many people before and after have meditated upon.

During all this time Mr. Spillikins was nerving himself to propose to Dulphemia Rasselyer-Brown. In fact, he spent part of his time walking up and down under the trees with Philippa Furlong and discussing with her the proposal that he meant to make, together with such topics as marriage in general and his own unworthiness.

He might have waited indefinitely had he not learned, on the third day of his visit, that Dulphemia was to go away in the morning to join her father at Nagahakett.

That evening he found the necessary nerve to speak, and the proposal in almost every aspect of it was most successful.

"By Jove!" Spillikins said to Philippa Furlong next morning, in explaining what had happened, "she was awfully nice about it. I think she must have guessed, in a way, don't you, what I was going to say? But at any rate she was awfully nice – let me say everything I wanted, and when I explained what a fool I was, she said she didn't think I was half such a fool as people thought me. But it's all right. It turns out that she isn't thinking of getting married. I asked her if I might always go on thinking of her, and she said I might."

And that morning when Dulphemia was carried off in the motor to the station, Mr. Spillikins, without exactly being aware how he had done it, had somehow transferred himself to Philippa.

"Isn't she a splendid girl!" he said at least ten times a day to Norah, the Little Girl in Green. And Norah always agreed, because she really thought Philippa a perfectly wonderful creature.

There is no doubt that, but for a slight shift of circumstances, Mr. Spillikins would have proposed to Miss Furlong. Indeed, he spent a good part of his time rehearsing little speeches that began, "Of course I know I'm an awful ass in a way," or, "Of course I know that I'm not at all the sort of fellow," and so on.

But not one of them ever was delivered.

For it so happened that on the Thursday, one week after Mr. Spillikins's arrival, Philippa went again to the station in the motor. And when she came back there was another passenger with her, a tall young man in tweed, and they both began calling out to the Newberrys from a distance of at least a hundred yards.

And both the Newberrys suddenly exclaimed, "Why, it's Tom!" and rushed off to meet the motor. And there was such a laughing and jubilation as the two descended and carried Tom's valises to the verandah, that Mr. Spillikins felt as suddenly and completely out of it as the Little Girl in Green herself – especially as his ear had caught, among the first things said, the words, "Congratulate us, Mrs. Newberry, we're engaged."

After which Mr. Spillikins had the pleasure of sitting and listening while it was explained, in wicker chairs on the verandah, that Philippa and Tom had been engaged already for ever so long – in fact, nearly two weeks, only they had agreed not to say a word to anybody till Tom had gone to North Carolina and back, to see his people.

And as to who Tom was, or what was the relation between Tom and the Newberrys, Mr. Spillikins neither knew nor cared; nor did it interest him in the least that Philippa had met Tom in Bermuda, and that she hadn't known that he even knew the Newberrys, nor any other of the exuberant disclosures of the moment. In fact, if there was any one period rather than another when Mr. Spillikins felt corroborated in his private view of himself, it was at this moment.

So the next day Tom and Philippa vanished together.

"We shall be quite a small party now," said Mrs. Newberry; "in fact, quite by ourselves till Mrs. Everleigh comes, and she won't be here for a fortnight."

At which the heart of the Little Girl in Green was glad, because she had been afraid that other girls might be coming, whereas she knew that Mrs. Everleigh was a widow with four sons and must be ever so old, past forty.

The next few days were spent by Mr. Spillikins almost entirely in the society of Norah. He thought them on the whole rather pleasant days, but slow. To her they were an uninterrupted dream of happiness never to be forgotten.

The Newberrys left them to themselves; not with any intent; it was merely that they were perpetually busy walking about the grounds of Castel Casteggio, blowing up things with dynamite, throwing steel bridges over gullies, and hoisting heavy timber with derricks. Nor were they to blame for it. For it had not always been theirs to command dynamite and control the forces of nature. There had been a time, now long ago, when the two Newberrys had lived, both of them, on twenty dollars a week, and Mrs. Newberry had made her own dresses, and Mr. Newberry had spent vigorous evenings in making hand-made shelves for their sitting-room. That was long ago, and since then Mr. Newberry, like many other people of those earlier days, had risen to wealth and Castel Casteggio, while others, like Norah's father, had stayed just where they were.

So the Newberrys left Peter and Norah to themselves all day. Even after dinner, in the evening, Mr. Newberry was very apt to call to his wife in the dusk from some distant corner of the lawn:

"Margaret, come over here and tell me if you don't think we

might cut down this elm, tear the stump out by the roots, and throw it into the ravine."

And the answer was, "One minute, Edward; just wait till I get a wrap."

Before they came back the dusk had grown to darkness, and they had redynamited half the estate.

During all of which time Mr. Spillikins sat with Norah on the piazza. He talked and she listened. He told her, for instance, all about his terrific experiences in the oil business, and about his exciting career at college; or presently they went indoors and Norah played the piano and Mr. Spillikins sat and smoked and listened. In such a house as the Newberrys', where dynamite and the greater explosives were everyday matters, a little thing like the use of tobacco in the drawing-room didn't count. As for the music, "Go right ahead," said Mr. Spillikins; "I'm not musical, but I don't mind music a bit."

In the daytime they played tennis. There was a court at one end of the lawn beneath the trees, all chequered with sunlight and mingled shadow; very beautiful, Norah thought, though Mr. Spillikins explained that the spotted light put him off his game. In fact, it was owing entirely to this bad light that Mr. Spillikins's fast drives, wonderful though they were, somehow never got inside the service court.

Norah, of course, thought Mr. Spillikins a wonderful player. She was glad – in fact, it suited them both – when he beat her six to nothing. She didn't know and didn't care that there was no one else in the world that Mr. Spillikins could beat like that. Once he even said to her,

"By Gad! you don't play half a bad game, you know. I think, you know, with practice you'd come on quite a lot."

After that the games were understood to be more or less in the form of lessons, which put Mr. Spillikins on a pedestal of superiority, and allowed any bad strokes on his part to be viewed as a form of indulgence.

Also, as the tennis was viewed in this light, it was Norah's part to pick up the balls at the net and throw them back to Mr. Spillikins. He let her do this, not from rudeness, for it wasn't in him, but because in such a primeval place as Castel Casteggio the natural primitive relation of the sexes is bound to reassert itself.

But of love Mr. Spillikins never thought. He had viewed it so eagerly and so often from a distance that when it stood here modestly at his very elbow he did not recognise its presence. His mind had been fashioned, as it were, to connect love with something stunning and sensational, with Easter hats and harem skirts and the luxurious consciousness of the unattainable.

Even at that, there is no knowing what might have happened. Tennis, in the chequered light of sun and shadow cast by summer leaves, is a dangerous game. There came a day when they were standing one each side of the net and Mr. Spillikins was explaining to Norah the proper way to hold a racquet so as to be able to give those magnificent backhand sweeps of his, by which he generally drove the ball half-way to the lake; and explaining this involved putting his hand right over Norah's on the handle of the racquet, so that for just half a second her hand was clasped tight in his; and if that half-second had been lengthened out into a whole second it is quite possible that what was already subconscious in his mind would have broken its way triumphantly to the surface, and Norah's hand would have stayed in his – how willingly! – for the rest of their two lives.

But just at that moment Mr. Spillikins looked up, and he said in quite an altered tone,

"By Jove! who's that awfully good-looking woman getting out of the motor?"

And their hands unclasped. Norah looked over towards the house and said,

"Why it's Mrs. Everleigh. I thought she wasn't coming for another week."

"I say," said Mr. Spillikins, straining his short sight to the uttermost, "what perfectly wonderful golden hair, eh?"

"Why, it's –" Norah began, and then she stopped. It didn't seem right to explain that Mrs. Everleigh's hair was dyed.

"And who's that tall chap standing beside her?" said Mr. Spillikins.

"I think it's Captain Cormorant, but I don't think he's going to stay. He's only brought her up in the motor from town."

"By Jove, how good of him!" said Spillikins; and this sentiment in regard to Captain Cormorant, though he didn't know it, was to become a keynote of his existence.

"I didn't know she was coming so soon," said Norah, and there was weariness already in her heart. Certainly she didn't know it; still less did she know, or anyone else, that the reason of Mrs. Everleigh's coming was because Mr. Spillikins was there. She came with a set purpose, and she sent Captain Cormorant directly back in the motor because she didn't want him on the premises.

"Oughtn't we to go up to the house?" said Norah.

"All right," said Mr. Spillikins with great alacrity, "let's go."

Now as this story began with the information that Mrs. Everleigh is at present Mrs. Everleigh-Spillikins, there is no need to pursue in detail the stages of Mr. Spillikins's wooing. Its course was swift and happy. Mr. Spillikins, having seen the back of Mrs. Everleigh's head, had decided instanter that she was the most beautiful woman in the world; and that impression is not easily corrected in the half-light of a shaded drawing-room; nor across a dinner-table lighted only with candles with deep red shades; nor even in the daytime through a veil. In any case, it is only fair to state that if Mrs. Everleigh was not and is not a singularly beautiful woman, Mr. Spillikins still doesn't know it. And in point of attraction the homage of such experts as Captain Cormorant and Lieutenant Hawk speaks for itself.

So the course of Mr. Spillikins's love, for love it must have been, ran swiftly to its goal. Each stage of it was duly marked by his comments to Norah.

"She *is* a splendid woman," he said, "so sympathetic. She always seems to know just what one's going to say."

So she did, for she was making him say it.

"By Jove!" he said a day later, "Mrs. Everleigh's an awfully fine woman, isn't she? I was telling her about my having been in the oil business for a little while, and she thinks that I'd really be awfully good in money things. She said she wished she had me to manage her money for her."

This also was quite true, except that Mrs. Everleigh had not made it quite clear that the management of her money was of the form generally known as deficit financing. In fact, her money was, very crudely stated, non-existent, and it needed a lot of management.

A day or two later Mr. Spillikins was saying, "I think Mrs. Everleigh must have had great sorrow, don't you? Yesterday she was showing me a photograph of her little boy – she has a little boy, you know –"

"Yes, I know," said Norah. She didn't add that she knew that Mrs. Everleigh had four.

"– and she was saying how awfully rough it is having to have him always away from her at Dr. Something's academy where he is."

And very soon after that Mr. Spillikins was saying, with quite a quaver in his voice,

"By Jove! yes, I'm awfully lucky; I never thought for a moment that she'd have me, you know – a woman like her, with so much attention and everything. I can't imagine what she sees in me."

Which was just as well.

And then Mr. Spillikins checked himself, for he noticed –

this was on the verandah in the morning – that Norah had a hat and jacket on and that the motor was rolling towards the door.

"I say," he said, "are you going away?"

"Yes, didn't you know?" Norah said. "I thought you heard them speaking of it at dinner last night. I have to go home; father's alone, you know."

"Oh, I'm awfully sorry," said Mr. Spillikins; "we shan't have any more tennis."

"Good-bye," said Norah, and as she said it and put out her hand there were tears brimming up into her eyes. But Mr. Spillikins, being short of sight, didn't see them.

"Good-bye," he said.

Then as the motor carried her away he stood for a moment in a sort of reverie. Perhaps certain things that might have been rose unformed and inarticulate before his mind. And then a voice called from the drawing-room within, in a measured and assured tone,

"Peter, darling, where are you?"

"Coming," cried Mr. Spillikins, and he came.

On the second day of the engagement Mrs. Everleigh showed to Peter a little photograph in a brooch.

"This is Gib, my second little boy," she said.

Mr. Spillikins started to say, "I didn't know –" and then checked himself and said, "By Gad! what a fine-looking little chap, eh? I'm awfully fond of boys."

"Dear little fellow, isn't he?" said Mrs. Everleigh. "He's really rather taller than that now, because this picture was taken a little while ago."

And the next day she said, "This is Willie, my third boy," and on the day after that she said, "This is Sib, my youngest boy; I'm sure you'll love him."

"I'm sure I shall," said Mr. Spillikins. He loved him already for being the youngest.

And so in the fulness of time – nor was it so very full either, in fact, only about five weeks – Peter Spillikins and Mrs. Everleigh were married in St. Asaph's Church on Plutoria Avenue. And the wedding was one of the most beautiful and sumptuous of the weddings of the September season. There were flowers, and bridesmaids in long veils, and tall ushers in frock-coats, and awnings at the church door, and strings of motors with wedding-favours on imported chauffeurs, and all that goes to invest marriage on Plutoria Avenue with its peculiar sacredness. The face of the young rector, Mr. Fareforth Furlong, wore the added saintliness that springs from the five-hundred dollar fee. The whole town was there, or at least everybody that was anybody, and if there was one person absent, one who sat by herself in the darkened drawing-room of a dull little house on a shabby street, who knew or cared?

So after the ceremony the happy couple – for were they not so? – left for New York. There they spent their honeymoon. They had thought of going, – it was Mr. Spillikins's idea, – to the coast of Maine. But Mrs. Everleigh-Spillikins said that New York was much nicer, so restful, whereas, as everyone knows, the coast of Maine is frightfully noisy.

Moreover, it so happened that before the Everleigh-Spillikinses had been more than four or five days in New York the ship of Captain Cormorant dropped anchor in the Hudson; and when the anchor of that ship was once down it generally stayed there. So the captain was able to take the Everleigh-Spillikinses about in New York, and to give a tea for Mrs. Everleigh-Spillikins on the deck of his vessel so that she might meet the officers, and another tea in a private room

of a restaurant on Fifth Avenue so that she might meet no on
but himself.

And at this tea Captain Cormorant said, among othe
things, "Did he kick up rough at all when you told him abou
the money?"

And Mrs. Everleigh, now Mrs. Everleigh-Spillikins said
"Not he! I think he is actually pleased to know that I haven'
any. Do you know, Arthur, he's really an awfully good fellow,
and as she said it she moved her hand away from unde
Captain Cormorant's on the tea-table.

"I say," said the Captain, "don't get sentimental over him."

So that is how it is that the Everleigh-Spillikinses came to
reside on Plutoria Avenue in a beautiful stone house, with the
billiard-room in an extension on the second floor. Through
the windows of it one can almost hear the click of the billiard
balls, and a voice saying, "Hold on, father, you had your shot."

(1914)

The Reading Public:

A Book Store Study

"WISH TO look about the store? Oh, by all means, sir," he said.

Then, as he rubbed his hands together in an urbane fashion, he directed a piercing glance at me through his spectacles.

"You'll find some things that might interest you," he said, "in the back of the store on the left. We have there a series of reprints – *Universal Knowledge from Aristotle to Arthur Balfour*, at seventeen cents. Or perhaps you might like to look over the *Pantheon of Dead Authors*, at ten cents. Mr. Sparrow," he called, "just show this gentleman our classical reprints – the ten-cent series."

With that he waved his hand to an assistant and dismissed me from his thought.

In other words, he had divined me in a moment. There was no use in my having bought a sage-green fedora in Broadway, and a sporting tie done up crosswise with spots as big as nickels. These little adornments can never hide the soul within. I was a professor, and he knew it, or at least, as part of his business, he could divine it on the instant.

The sales manager of the biggest book store for ten blocks cannot be deceived in a customer. And he knew, of course, that, as a professor, I was no good. I had come to the store, as

83

all professors go to book stores, just as a wasp comes to an open jar of marmalade. He knew that I would hang around for two hours, get in everybody's way, and finally buy a cheap reprint of the *Dialogues of Plato*, or the *Prose Works of John Milton*, or *Locke on the Human Understanding*, or some trash of that sort.

As for real taste in literature – the ability to appreciate at its worth a dollar-fifty novel of last month, in a spring jacket with a tango frontispiece – I hadn't got it and he knew it.

He despised me, of course. But it is a maxim of the book business that a professor standing up in a corner buried in a book looks well in a store. The real customers like it.

So it was that even so up-to-date a manager as Mr. Sellyer tolerated my presence in a back corner of his store; and so it was that I had an opportunity of noting something of his methods with his real customers – methods so successful, I may say, that he is rightly looked upon by all the publishing business as one of the mainstays of literature in America.

I had no intention of standing in the place and listening as a spy. In fact, to tell the truth, I had become immediately interested in a new translation of the *Moral Discourses of Epictetus*. The book was very neatly printed, quite well bound and was offered at eighteen cents; so that for the moment I was strongly tempted to buy it, though it seemed best to take a dip into it first.

I had hardly read more than the first three chapters when my attention was diverted by a conversation going on in the front of the store.

"You're quite sure it's his *latest*?" a fashionably dressed woman was saying to Mr. Sellyer.

"Oh, yes, Mrs. Rasselyer," answered the manager. "I assure you this is his very latest. In fact, they only came in yesterday."

As he spoke, he indicated with his hand a huge pile of books, gaily jacketed in white and blue. I could make out the title in big gilt lettering – *GOLDEN DREAMS*.

"Oh, yes," repeated Mr. Sellyer. "This is Mr. Slush's latest book. It's having a wonderful sale."

"That's all right, then," said the lady. "You see, one sometimes gets taken in so: I came in here last week and took two that seemed very nice, and I never noticed till I got home that they were both old books, published, I think, six months ago."

"Oh, dear me, Mrs. Rasselyer," said the manager in an apologetic tone, "I'm extremely sorry. Pray let us send for them and exchange them for you."

"Oh, it does not matter," said the lady. "Of course I didn't read them. I gave them to my maid. She probably wouldn't know the difference, anyway."

"I suppose not," said Mr. Sellyer, with a condescending smile. "But of course, madam," he went on, falling into the easy chat of the fashionable bookman, "such mistakes are bound to happen sometimes. We had a very painful case only yesterday. One of our oldest customers came in, in a great hurry, to buy books to take on the steamer, and before we realized what he had done – selecting the books I suppose merely by the titles, as some gentlemen are apt to do – he had taken two of last year's books. We wired at once to the steamer, but I'm afraid it's too late."

"But now, this book," said the lady, idly turning over the leaves, "is it good? What is it about?"

"It's an extremely *powerful* thing," said Mr. Sellyer, "in fact, *masterly*. The critics are saying that it's perhaps *the* most powerful book of the season. It has a —" and here Mr. Sellyer paused, and somehow his manner reminded me of my own when I am explaining to a university class something that I don't know myself. "It has a – a – *power*, so to speak, a very exceptional power; in fact, one may say without exaggeration it is the most *powerful* book of the month. Indeed," he added, getting on to easier ground, "it's having a perfectly wonderful sale."

"You seem to have a great many of them," said the lady.

"Oh, we have to," answered the manager. "There's a regular rush on the book. Indeed, you know it's a book that is bound to make a sensation. In fact, in certain quarters, they are saying that it's a book that ought not to —" And here Mr. Sellyer's voice became so low and ingratiating that I couldn't hear the rest of the sentence.

"Oh, really!" said Mrs. Rasselyer. "Well, I think I'll take it then. One ought to see what these talked-of things are about, anyway."

She had already begun to button her gloves, and to readjust her feather boa, with which she had been knocking the Easter cards off the counter. Then she suddenly remembered something.

"Oh, I was forgetting," she said. "Will you send something to the house for Mr. Rasselyer at the same time? He's going down to Virginia for the vacation. You know the kind of thing he likes, do you not?"

"Oh, perfectly, madam," said the manager. "Mr. Rasselyer generally reads works of – er – I think he buys mostly books on – er —"

"Oh, travel and that sort of thing," said the lady.

"Precisely. I think we have here," and he pointed to the counter on the left, "what Mr. Rasselyer wants" – he indicated a row of handsome books – "*Seven Weeks in the Sahara*, seven dollars; *Six Months in a Waggon*, six-fifty net; *Afternoons in an Ox-cart*, two volumes, four-thirty, with twenty off."

"I think he has read those," said Mrs. Rasselyer. "At least there are a good many at home that seem like that."

"Oh, very possibly. But here, now, *Among the Cannibals of Corfu* – yes, that I think he has had – *Among the* – that, too, I think. But this I am certain he would like, just in this morning, *Among the Monkeys of New Guinea*, ten dollars, net."

And with this Mr. Sellyer laid his hand on a pile of new books, apparently as numerous as the huge pile of *Golden Dreams*.

"*Among the Monkeys*," he repeated, almost caressingly.

"It seems rather expensive," said the lady.

"Oh, very much so – a most expensive book," the manager repeated in a tone of enthusiasm. "You see, Mrs. Rasselyer, it's the illustrations, actual photographs" – he ran the leaves over in his – fingers – "of actual monkeys, taken with the camera; and the paper, you notice. In fact, madam, the book costs, the mere manufacture of it, nine dollars and ninety cents. Of course we make no profit on it; but it's a book we like to handle."

Everybody likes to be taken into the details of technical business; and of course everybody likes to know that a bookseller is losing money. These, I realized, were two axioms in the methods of Mr. Sellyer.

So very naturally Mrs. Rasselyer bought *Among the Monkeys*, and in another moment Mr. Sellyer was directing a clerk to write down an address on Fifth Avenue, and was bowing deeply as he showed the lady out of the door.

As he turned back to his counter his manner seemed much changed.

"That Monkey book," I heard him murmur to his assistant, "is going to be a pretty stiff proposition."

But he had no time for further speculation.

Another lady entered.

This time, even to an eye less trained than Mr. Sellyer's, the deep, expensive mourning and the pensive face proclaimed the sentimental widow.

"Something new in fiction," repeated the manager, "yes, madam, here's a charming thing, *Golden Dreams*" – he hung lovingly on the words – "a very sweet story, singularly sweet; in fact, madam, the critics are saying it is the sweetest thing that Mr. Slush has done."

"Is it good?" said the lady.

I began to realize that all customers asked this.

"A charming book," said the manager. "It's a love story –

very simple and sweet, yet wonderfully charming. Indeed, the reviews say it's the most charming book of the month. My wife was reading it aloud only last night. She could hardly read for tears."

"I suppose it's quite a safe book, is it?" asked the widow. "I want it for my little daughter."

"Oh, quite safe," said Mr. Sellyer, with an almost parental tone, "in fact, written quite in the old style, like the dear old books of the past; quite like" – here Mr. Sellyer paused with a certain slight haze of doubt visible in his eye – "Dickens and Fielding and Sterne and so on. We sell a great many to the clergy, madam."

The lady bought *Golden Dreams*, received it wrapped up in green enamelled paper, and passed out.

"Have you any good light reading for vacation time?" called out the next customer in a loud, breezy voice – he had the air of a stockbroker starting on a holiday.

"Yes," said Mr. Sellyer, and his face almost broke into a laugh as he answered, "here's an excellent thing, *Golden Dreams*; quite the most humorous book of the season – simply screaming – my wife was reading it aloud only yesterday. She could hardly read for laughing."

"What's the price, one dollar? One-fifty. All right, wrap it up."

There was a clink of money on the counter, and the customer was gone. I began to see exactly where professors and college people who want copies of *Epictetus* at eighteen cents and sections of *World Reprints of Literature* at twelve cents a section come in, in the book trade.

"Yes, Judge," said the manager to the next customer, a huge, dignified personage in a wide-awake hat, "sea stories? Certainly. Excellent reading, no doubt, when the brain is overcharged as yours must be. Here is the very latest, *Among the Monkeys of New Guinea*, ten dollars, reduced to four-fifty. The manufacture alone costs six-eighty. We're selling it out. Thank you, Judge. Send it? Yes. Good morning."

After that the customers came and went in a string. I noticed that though the store was filled with books – ten thousand of them, at a guess – Mr. Sellyer was apparently only selling two. Every woman who entered went away with *Golden Dreams*; every man was given a copy of the *Monkeys of New Guinea*. To one lady *Golden Dreams* was sold as exactly the reading for a holiday, to another as the very book to read *after* a holiday; another bought it as a book for a rainy day, and a fourth as the right sort of reading for a fine day. The Monkeys was sold as a sea story, a land story, a story of the jungle, and a story of the mountains, and it was put at a price corresponding to Mr. Sellyer's estimate of the purchaser.

At last after a busy two hours, the store grew empty for a moment.

"Wilfred," said Mr. Sellyer, turning to his chief assistant, "I am going out to lunch. Keep those two books running as hard as you can. We'll try them for another day and then cut them right out. And I'll drop round to Dockem and Discount, the publishers, and make a kick about them, and see what they'll do."

I felt that I had lingered long enough. I drew near with the *Epictetus* in my hand.

"Yes, sir," said Mr. Sellyer, professional again in a moment. "*Epictetus*? A charming thing. Eighteen cents. Thank you. Perhaps we have some other things there that might interest you. We have a few second-hand things in the alcove there that you might care to look at. There's an *Aristotle*, two volumes, a very fine thing, practically illegible, that you might like; and a *Cicero* came in yesterday, very choice, damaged by damp; and I think we have a *Machiavelli*, quite exceptional, practically torn to pieces, and the covers gone. A very rare old thing, sir, if you're an expert."

"No, thanks," I said. And then from a curiosity that had been growing in me and that I couldn't resist, "That book – *Golden Dreams*," I said, "you seem to think it a very wonderful work?"

Mr. Sellyer directed one of his shrewd glances at me. He knew I didn't want to buy the book, and perhaps, like lesser people, he had his off moments of confidence.

He shook his head.

"A bad business," he said. "The publishers have unloaded the thing on us, and we have to do what we can. They're stuck with it, I understand, and they look to us to help them. They're advertising it largely and may pull it off. Of course, there's just a chance. One can't tell. It's just possible we may get the church people down on it and if so we're all right. But short of that we'll never make it. I imagine it's perfectly rotten."

"Haven't you read it?" I asked.

"Dear me, no!" said the manager. His air was that of a milk-man who is offered a glass of his own milk. "A pretty time I'd have if I tried to *read* the new books. It's quite enough to keep track of them without that."

"But those people," I went on, deeply perplexed, "who bought the book. Won't they be disappointed?"

Mr. Sellyer shook his head. "Oh, no," he said. "You see, they won't *read* it. They never do."

"But at any rate," I insisted, "your wife thought it a fine story."

Mr. Sellyer smiled widely.

"I am not married, sir," he said.

(1915)

The Snoopopaths

or Fifty Stories in One

THIS PARTICULAR study in the follies of literature is not so much a story as a sort of essay. The average reader will therefore turn from it with a shudder. The condition of the average reader's mind is such that he can take in nothing but fiction. And it must be thin fiction at that – thin as gruel. Nothing else will "sit on his stomach."

Everything must come to the present day reader in this form. If you wish to talk to him about religion, you must dress it up as a story and label it *Beth-sheba, or The Curse of David*; if you want to improve the reader's morals, you must write him a little thing in dialogue called *Mrs. Potiphar Dines Out*. If you wish to expostulate with him about drink you must do so through a narrative called *Red Rum* – short enough and easy enough for him to read it, without overstraining his mind, while he drinks cocktails.

But whatever the story is about it has got to deal – in order to be read by the average reader – with *A MAN* and *A WOMAN*. I put these words in capitals to indicate that they have got to stick out of the story with the crudity of a drawing done by a child with a burnt stick. In other words, the story has got to be snoopopathic. This is a word derived from the Greek – "snoopo" – or if there never was a Greek verb snoopo, at least there ought to have been one – and it means just what it seems to mean. Nine out of ten short stories written in America are snoopopathic.

In snoopopathic literature, in order to get its full effect, the writer generally introduces his characters simply as "the man" and "the woman." He hates to admit that they have names. He opens out with them something after this fashion:

"The Man lifted his head. He looked about him at the gaily-bedizzled crowd that besplotched the midnight cabaret with riotous patches of colour. He crushed his cigar against the brass of an Egyptian tray – 'Bah!' he murmured, 'Is it worth it?' Then he let his head sink again."

You notice it? He lifted his head all the way up and let it sink all the way down, and you still don't know who he is.

For The Woman the beginning is done like this:

"The Woman clenched her white hands till the diamonds that glittered upon her fingers were buried in the soft flesh. 'The shame of it,' she murmured. Then she took from the table the telegram that lay crumpled upon it and tore it into a hundred pieces. 'He dare not!' she muttered through her closed teeth. She looked about the hotel room with its garish furniture. 'He has no right to follow me here,' she gasped."

All of which the reader has to take in without knowing who the woman is, or which hotel she is staying at, or who dare not follow her or why. But the modern reader loves to get this sort of shadowy incomplete effect. If he were told straight out that the woman's name was Mrs. Edward Dangerfield of Brick City, Montana, and that she had left her husband three days ago and that the telegram told her that he had discovered her address and was following her, the reader would refuse to go on.

This method of introducing the characters is bad enough. But the new snoopopathic way of describing them is still worse. The Man is always detailed as if he were a horse. He is said to be "tall, well set up, with straight legs."

Great stress is always laid on his straight legs. No magazine story is acceptable now unless The Man's legs are absolutely straight. Why this is, I don't know. All my friends have straight legs – and yet I never hear them make it a subject of comment or boasting. I don't believe I have, at present, a single friend with crooked legs.

But this is not the only requirement. Not only must The Man's legs be straight, but he must be "clean-limbed," whatever that is; and of course he must have a "well-tubbed look about him." How this look is acquired, and whether it can be got with an ordinary bath and water, are things on which I have no opinion.

The Man is of course "clean-shaven." This allows him to do such necessary things as "turning his clean-shaven face towards the speaker," "laying his clean-shaven cheek in his hand," and so on. But every one is familiar with the face of the up-to-date clean-shaven snoopopathic man. There are pictures of him by the million on magazine covers and book jackets, looking into the eyes of The Woman – he does it from a distance of about six inches – with that snoopy earnest expression of brainlessness that he always wears. How one would enjoy seeing a man – a real one with Nevada whiskers and long boots – land him one solid kick from behind.

Then comes The Woman of the snoopopathic story. She is always "beautifully groomed" (Who these grooms are that do it, and where they can be hired, I don't know), and she is said to be "exquisitely gowned."

It is peculiar about The Woman that she never seems to wear a *dress* – always a "gown." Why this is, I cannot tell. In the good old stories that I used to read, when I could still read for the pleasure of it, the heroines – that was what they used to be called – always wore dresses. But now there is no heroine, only a woman in a gown. I wear a gown myself – at night. It is made of flannel and reaches to my feet, and when I take my candle and go out to the balcony where I sleep, the effect of it on the whole is not bad. But as to its "revealing every line of my figure" – as The Woman's gown is always said to – and as to its "suggesting even more than it reveals" – well, it simply does *not*. So when I talk of "gowns" I speak of something that I know all about.

Yet whatever The Woman does, her "gown" is said to "cling" to her. Whether in the street or in a cabaret or in the drawing-room, it "clings." If by any happy chance she throws a lace wrap about her, then *it* clings; and if she lifts her gown – as she is apt to – it shows – not what I should have expected – but a *jupon*, and even that clings. What a *jupon* is I don't know. With my gown, I never wear one. These people I have described, The Man and The Woman – The Snoopopaths – are, of course, not husband and wife, or brother and sister, or anything so simple and old-fashioned as that. She is some one else's wife. She is *The Wife of the Other Man*. Just what there is, for the reader, about other men's wives, I don't understand. I know tons of them that I wouldn't walk round a block for. But the reading public goes wild over them. The old-fashioned heroine was unmarried. That spoiled the whole story. You could see the end from the beginning. But with Another Man's Wife, the way is blocked. Something has *got* to happen that would seem almost obvious to any one.

The writer, therefore, at once puts the two snoopos – The Man and The Woman – into a frightfully indelicate position. The more indelicate it is, the better. Sometimes she gets into his motor by accident after the theatre, or they both engage the drawing-room of a Pullman car by mistake, or else, best of all, he is brought accidentally into her room at a hotel at night. There is something about a hotel room at night, apparently, which throws the modern reader into convulsions. It is always easy to arrange a scene of this sort. For example, taking the sample beginning that I gave above, The Man – whom I left sitting at the cabaret table, above, rises unsteadily – it is the recognised way of rising in a cabaret – and, settling the reckoning with the waiter, staggers into the street. For myself I never do a reckoning with the waiter. I just pay the bill as he adds it, and take a chance on it.

As The Man staggers into the "night air," the writer has time – just a little time, for the modern reader is impatient – to explain who he is and why he staggers. He is rich. That goes without saying. All clean-limbed men with straight legs are rich. He owns copper mines in Montana. All well-tubbed millionaires do. But he has left them, left everything, because of the Other Man's Wife. It was that or madness – or worse. He had told himself so a thousand times. (This little touch about "worse" is used in all the stories. I don't just understand what the "worse" means. But snoopopathic readers reach for it with great readiness.) So The Man had come to New York (the only place where stories are allowed to be laid) under an assumed name, to forget, to drive her from his mind. He had plunged into the mad round of – I never could find it myself, but it must be there, and as they all plunge into it, it must be as full of them as a sheet of Tanglefoot is of flies.

"As The Man walked home to his hotel, the cool, night air steadied him, but his brain is still filled with the fumes of the wine he had drunk." Notice these "fumes." It must be great to float round with them in one's brain, where they apparently lodge. I have often tried to find them, but I never can. Again and again I have said, "Waiter, bring me a Scotch whiskey and soda with fumes." But I can never get them.

Thus goes The Man to his hotel. Now it is in a room in this same hotel that The Woman is sitting, and in which she has crumpled up the telegram. It is to this hotel that she has come when she left her husband, a week ago. The readers know, without even being told, that she left him "to work out her own salvation" – driven, by his cold brutality, beyond the breaking point. And there is laid upon her soul, as she sits there with clenched hands, the dust and ashes of a broken marriage and a loveless life, and the knowledge, too late, of all that might have been.

And it is to this hotel that The Woman's Husband is following her.

But The Man does not know that she is in the hotel; nor that she has left her husband; it is only accident that brings them together. And it is only by accident that he has come into her room, at night, and stands there – rooted to the threshold.

Now as a matter of fact, in real life, there is nothing at all in the simple fact of walking into the wrong room of a hotel by accident. You merely apologise and go out. I had this experience myself only a few days ago. I walked right into a lady's room – next door to my own. But I simply said, "Oh, I beg your pardon, I thought this was No. 343."

"No," she said, "this is 341."

She did not rise and "confront" me, as they always do in the snoopopathic stories. Neither did her eyes flash, nor her gown cling to her as she rose. Nor was her gown made of "rich old stuff." No, she merely went on reading her newspaper.

"I must apologise," I said. "I am a little short-sighted, and very often a *one* and a *three* look so alike that I can't tell them apart. I'm afraid —"

"Not at all," said the lady. "Good evening."

"You see," I added, "this room and my own being so alike, and mine being 343 and this being 341, I walked in before I realised that instead of walking into 343 I was walking into 341."

She bowed in silence, without speaking, and I felt that it was now the part of exquisite tact to retire quietly without further explanation, or at least with only a few murmured words about the possibility of to-morrow being even colder than to-day. I did so, and the affair ended with complete *savoir faire* on both sides.

But the Snoopopaths, Man and Woman, can't do this sort of thing, or, at any rate, the snoopopathic writer won't let them. The opportunity is too good to miss. As soon as The Man comes into The Woman's room – before he knows who she is, for she has her back to him – he gets into a condition dear to all snoopopathic readers.

His veins simply "surged." His brain beat against his temples in mad pulsation. His breath "came and went in quick, short pants." (This last might perhaps be done by one of the hotel bellboys, but otherwise it is hard to imagine.)

And The Woman – "Noiseless as his step had been she seemed to *sense* his presence. A wave seemed to sweep over her —" She turned and rose "fronting him full." This doesn't mean that he was full when she fronted him. Her gown – but we know about that already. "It was a coward's trick," she panted.

Now if The Man had had the kind of *savoir faire* that I have, he would have said: "Oh, pardon me! I see this room is 341. My own room is 343, and to me a *one* and a *three* often look so alike that I seem to have walked into 341 while looking for 343." And he could have explained in two words that he had no idea that she was in New York, was not following her, and not proposing to interfere with her in any way. And she would have explained also in two sentences why and how she came to be there. But this wouldn't do. Instead of it, The Man and The Woman go through the grand snoopopathic scene which is so intense that it needs what is really a new kind of language to convey it.

"Helene," he croaked, reaching out his arms – his voice tensed with the infinity of his desire.

"Back," she iced. And then, "Why have you come here?" she hoarsed. "What business have you here?"

"None," he glooped, "none. I have no business." They stood sensing one another.

"I thought you were in Philadelphia," she said – her gown clinging to every fibre of her as she spoke.

"I was," he wheezed.

"And you left it?" she sharped, her voice tense.

"I left it," he said, his voice glumping as he spoke. "Need I tell you why?" He had come nearer to her. She could hear his pants as he moved.

"No, no," she gurgled. "You left it. It is enough. I can under-stand" – she looked bravely up at him – "I can understand any man leaving it." Then as he moved still nearer her, there was the sound of a sudden swift step in the corridor. The door opened and there stood before them – The Other Man, the Husband of The Woman – Edward Dangerfield.

This, of course, is the grand snoopopathic climax, when the author gets all three of them – The Man, The Woman, and The Woman's Husband – in a hotel room at night. But notice what happens.

He stood in the opening of the doorway looking at them, a slight smile upon his lips. "Well?" he said. Then he entered the room and stood for a moment quietly looking into The Man's face.

"So," he said, "it was you." He walked into the room and laid the light coat that he had been carrying over his arm upon the table. He drew a cigar case from his waistcoat pocket.

"Try one of these Havanas," he said.

Observe the *calm* of it. This is what the snoopopath loves – no rage, no blustering – calmness, cynicism. He walked over towards the mantel-piece and laid his hat upon it. He set his boot upon the fender.

"It was cold this evening," he said. He walked over to the window and gazed a moment into the dark.

"This is a nice hotel," he said. (This scene is what the author and the reader love; they hate to let it go. They'd willingly keep the man walking up and down for hours saying "Well!")

The Man raised his head! "Yes, it's a good hotel," he said. Then he let his head fall again.

This kind of thing goes on until, if possible, the reader is persuaded into thinking that there is nothing going to happen. Then: –

"He turned to The Woman. 'Go in there,' he said, pointing

to the bedroom door. Mechanically she obeyed." This, by the way, is the first intimation that the reader has that the room in which they were sitting was not a bedroom. The two men were alone. Dangerfield walked over to the chair where he had thrown his coat.

"I bought this coat in St. Louis last fall," he said. His voice was quiet, even passionless. Then from the pocket of the coat he took a revolver and laid it on the table. Marsden watched him without a word.

"Do you see this pistol?" said Dangerfield.

Marsden raised his head a moment and let it sink.

Of course the ignorant reader keeps wondering why he doesn't explain. But how can he? What is there to say? He has been found out of his own room at night. The penalty for this in all the snoopopathic stories is death. It is understood that in all the New York hotels the night porters shoot a certain number of men in the corridors every night.

"When we married," said Dangerfield, glancing at the closed door as he spoke, "I bought this and the mate to it – for her – just the same, with the monogram on the butt – see! And I said to her, 'If things ever go wrong between you and me, there is always this way out.'"

He lifted the pistol from the table, examining its mechanism. He rose and walked across the room till he stood with his back against the door, the pistol in his hand, its barrel pointing straight at Marsden's heart. Marsden never moved. Then as the two men faced one another thus, looking into one another's eyes, their ears caught a sound from behind the closed door of the inner room – a sharp, hard, metallic sound as if some one in the room within had raised the hammer of a pistol – a jewelled pistol like the one in Dangerfield's hand.

And then –

A loud report, and with a cry, the cry of a woman, one shrill despairing cry —

Or no, hang it – I can't consent to end up a story in that

fashion, with the dead woman prone across the bed, the smoking pistol, with a jewel on the hilt, still clasped in her hand – the red blood welling over the white laces of her gown – while the two men gaze down upon her cold face with horror in their eyes. Not a bit. Let's end it like this: –

"A shrill despairing cry, – 'Ed! Charlie! Come in here quick! Hurry! The steam coil has blown out a plug! You two boys quit talking and come in here, for Heaven's sake, and fix it.'"

And, indeed, if the reader will look back he will see there is nothing in the dialogue to preclude it. He was misled, that's all. I merely said that Mrs. Dangerfield had left her husband a few days before. So she had – to do some shopping in New York. She thought it mean of him to follow her. And I never said that Mrs. Dangerfield had any connection whatever with The Woman with whom Marsden was in love. Not at all. He knew her, of course, because he came from Brick City. But she had thought he was in Philadelphia, and naturally she was surprised to see him back in New York. That's why she exclaimed "Back!" And as a matter of plain fact, you can't pick up a revolver without its pointing somewhere. No one said he meant to fire it.

In fact, if the reader will glance back at the dialogue – I know he has no time to, but if he does – he will see that, being something of a snoopopath himself, he has invented the whole story.

(1916)

My Revelations as a Spy

IN MANY people the very name "Spy" excites a shudder of apprehension; we Spies, in fact, get quite used to being shuddered at. None of us Spies mind it at all. Whenever I enter a hotel and register myself as a Spy I am quite accustomed to see a thrill of fear run round the clerks, or clerk, behind the desk.

Us Spies or We Spies – for we call ourselves both – are thus a race apart. None know us. All fear us. Where do we live? Nowhere. Where are we? Everywhere. Frequently we don't know ourselves where we are. The secret orders that we receive come from so high up that it is often forbidden to us even to ask where we are. A friend of mine, or at least a Fellow Spy – us spies have no friends – one of the most brilliant men in the Hungarian Secret Service, once spent a month in New York under the impression that he was in Winnipeg. If this happened to the most brilliant, think of the others.

All, I say, fear us. Because they know and have reason to know our power. Hence, in spite of the prejudice against us, we are able to move everywhere, to lodge in the best hotels, and enter any society that we wish to penetrate.

Let me relate an incident to illustrate this: A month ago I entered one of the largest of the New York hotels which I will merely call the B. hotel without naming it: to do so might blast it. We spies, in fact, never *name* a hotel. At the most we indicate it by a number known only to ourselves, such as 1, 2, or 3.

On my presenting myself at the desk the clerk informed me that he had no room vacant. I knew this of course to be a mere subterfuge; whether or not he suspected that I was a spy I cannot say. I was muffled up, to avoid recognition, in a long overcoat with the collar turned up and reaching well above my ears, while the black beard and the moustache, that I had slipped on in entering the hotel, concealed my face. "Let me speak a moment to the manager," I said. When he came I beckoned him aside and taking his ear in my hand I breathed two words into it. "Good heavens!" he gasped, while his face turned as pale as ashes. "Is it enough?" I asked. "Can I have a room, or must I breathe again?" "No, no," said the manager, still trembling. Then, turning to the clerk: "Give this gentleman a room," he said, "and give him a bath."

What these two words are that will get a room in New York at once I must not divulge. Even now, when the veil of secrecy is being lifted, the international interests involved are too complicated to permit it. Suffice it to say that if these two had failed I know a couple of others still better.

I narrate this incident, otherwise trivial, as indicating the astounding ramifications and the ubiquity of the international spy system. A similar illustration occurs to me as I write. I was walking the other day with another gentleman – on upper B. way between the T. Building and the W. Garden.

"Do you see that man over there?" I said, pointing from the side of the street on which we were walking on the sidewalk to the other side opposite to the side that we were on.

"The man with the straw hat?" he asked. "Yes, what of him?"

"Oh, nothing," I answered, "except that he's a Spy!"

"Great heavens!" exclaimed my acquaintance leaning up against a lamppost for support. "A Spy! How do you know that? What does it mean?"

I gave a quiet laugh – we spies learn to laugh very quietly. "Ha!" I said, "that is *my* secret, my friend. *Verbum sapientius! Che sarà sarà! Yodel doodle doo!*"

My acquaintance fell in a dead faint upon the street. I watched them take him away in an ambulance. Will the reader be surprised to learn that among the white-coated attendants who removed him I recognised no less a person than the famous Russian spy Poulispantzoff. What he was doing there I could not tell. No doubt his orders came from so high up that he himself did not know. I had seen him only twice before – once when we were both disguised as Zulus at Buluwaye, and once in the interior of China, at the time when Poulispantzoff made his secret entry into Thibet concealed in a tea-case. He was inside the tea-case when I saw him; so at least I was informed by the coolies who carried it. Yet I recognised him instantly. Neither he nor I, however, gave any sign of recognition other than an imperceptible movement of the outer eyelid. (We spies learn to move the outer lid of the eye so imperceptibly that it cannot be seen.) Yet after meeting Poulispantzoff in this way I was not surprised to read in the evening papers a few hours afterward that the uncle of the young King of Siam had been assassinated. The connection between these two events I am unfortunately not at liberty to explain; the consequences to the Vatican would be too serious. I doubt if it could remain top-side up.

These, however, are but passing incidents in a life filled with danger and excitement. They would have remained unrecorded and unrevealed, like the rest of my revelations, were it not that certain recent events have to some extent removed the seal of secrecy from my lips. The death of a certain royal sovereign makes it possible for me to divulge things hitherto undivulgible. Even now I can only tell a part, a small part, of the terrific things that I know. When more sovereigns die I can divulge more. I hope to keep on divulging at intervals for years. But I am compelled to be cautious. My relations with the Wilhelmstrasse, with Downing Street and the Quai d'Orsay, are so intimate, and my footing with the Yildiz Kiosk and the Waldorf-Astoria and Childs' Restaurants are so delicate, that a single *faux pas* might prove to be a false step.

It is now seventeen years since I entered the Secret Service of the G. empire. During this time my activities have taken me into every quarter of the globe, at times even into every eighth or sixteenth of it. It was I who first brought back word to the Imperial Chancellor of the existence of an Entente between England and France. "Is there an entente?" he asked me, trembling with excitement, on my arrival at the Wilhelmstrasse. "Your Excellency," I said, "there is." He groaned. "Can you stop it?" he asked.

"Don't ask me," I said sadly. "Where must we strike?" demanded the Chancellor. "Fetch me a map," I said. They did so. I placed my finger on the map. "Quick, quick," said the Chancellor, "look where his finger is." They lifted it up. "Morocco!" they cried. I had meant it for Abyssinia but it was too late to change. That night the warship *Panther* sailed under sealed orders. The rest is history, or at least history and geography.

In the same way it was I who brought word to the Wilhelmstrasse of the *rapprochement* between England and Russia in Persia. "What did you find?" asked the Chancellor as I laid aside the Russian disguise in which I had travelled. "A *Rapprochement*!" I said. He groaned. "They seem to get all the best words," he said.

I shall always feel, to my regret, that I am personally responsible for the outbreak of the present war. It may have had ulterior causes. But there is no doubt that it was precipitated by the fact that, for the first time in seventeen years, I took a six weeks' vacation in June and July of 1914. The consequences of this careless step I ought to have foreseen. Yet I took such precautions as I could. "Do you think," I asked, "that you can preserve the status quo for six weeks, merely six weeks, if I stop spying and take a rest?" "We'll try," they answered. "Remember," I said, as I packed my things, "keep the Dardanelles closed; have the Sandjak of Novi Bazaar properly patrolled, and let the Dobrudja remain under a *modus vivendi* till I come back."

Two months later, while sitting sipping my coffee at a Kurhof in the Schwarzwald, I read in the newspapers that a German army had invaded France and was fighting the French, and that the English expeditionary force had crossed the Channel. "This," I said to myself, "means war." As usual, I was right.

It is needless for me to recount here the life of busy activity that falls to a Spy in wartime. It was necessary for me to be here, there and everywhere, visiting all the best hotels, watering-places, summer resorts, theatres, and places of amusement. It was necessary, moreover, to act with the utmost caution and to assume an air of careless indolence in order to lull suspicion asleep. With this end in view I made a practice of never rising till ten in the morning. I breakfasted with great leisure, and contented myself with passing the morning in a quiet stroll, taking care, however, to keep my ears open. After lunch I generally feigned a light sleep, keeping my ears shut. A *table d'hôte* dinner, followed by a visit to the theatre, brought the strenuous day to a close. Few spies, I venture to say, worked harder than I did.

It was during the third year of the war that I received a peremptory summons from the head of the Imperial Secret Service at Berlin, Baron Fisch von Gestern. "I want to see you," it read. Nothing more. In the life of a Spy one learns to think quickly, and to think is to act. I gathered as soon as I received the despatch that for some reason or other Fisch von Gestern was anxious to see me, having, as I instantly inferred, something to say to me. This conjecture proved correct.

The Baron rose at my entrance with military correctness and shook hands.

"Are you willing," he inquired, "to undertake a mission to America?"

"I am," I answered.

"Very good. How soon can you start?"

"As soon as I have paid the few bills that I owe in Berlin," I replied.

"We can hardly wait for that," said my chief, "and in case it might excite comment. You must start to-night!"

"Very good," I said.

"Such," said the Baron, "are the Kaiser's orders. Here is an American passport and a photograph that will answer the purpose. The likeness is not great, but it is sufficient."

"But," I objected, abashed for a moment, "this photograph is of a man with whiskers and I am, unfortunately, clean-shaven."

"The orders are imperative," said von Gestern, with official hauteur. "You must start to-night. You can grow whiskers this afternoon."

"Very good," I replied.

"And now to the business of your mission," continued the Baron. "The United States, as you have perhaps heard, is making war against Germany."

"I have heard so," I replied.

"Yes," continued von Gestern. "The fact has leaked out, – how we do not know, – and is being widely reported. His Imperial Majesty has decided to stop the war with the United States." I bowed.

"He intends to send over a secret treaty of the same nature as the one recently made with his recent Highness the recent Czar of Russia. Under this treaty Germany proposes to give to the United States the whole of equatorial Africa and in return the United States is to give to Germany the whole of China.

There are other provisions, but I need not trouble you with them. Your mission relates, not to the actual treaty, but to the preparation of the ground." I bowed again.

"You are aware, I presume," continued the Baron, "that in all high international dealings, at least in Europe, the ground has to be prepared. A hundred threads must be unravelled. This the Imperial Government itself cannot stoop to do. The work must be done by agents like yourself. You understand all this already, no doubt?" I indicated my assent.

"These, then, are your instructions," said the Baron, speaking slowly and distinctly, as if to impress his words upon my memory. "On your arrival in the United States you will follow the accredited methods that are known to be used by all the best spies of the highest diplomacy. You have no doubt read some of the books, almost manuals of instruction, that they have written?"

"I have read many of them," I said.

"Very well. You will enter, that is to say, enter and move everywhere in the best society. Mark specially, please, that you must not only *enter* it but you must *move*. You must, if I may put it so, get a move on." I bowed.

"You must mix freely with the members of the Cabinet. You must dine with them. This is a most necessary matter and one to be kept well in mind. Dine with them often in such a way as to make yourself familiar to them. Will you do this?"

"I will," I said.

"Very good. Remember also that in order to mask your purpose you must constantly be seen with the most fashionable and most beautiful women of the American capital. Can you do this?"

"Can I?" I said.

"You must if need be" – and the Baron gave a most significant look which was not lost upon me – "carry on an intrigue with one or, better, with several of them. Are you ready for it?"

"More than ready," I said.

"Very good. But this is only a part. You are expected also to familiarise yourself with the leaders of the great financial interests. You are to put yourself on such a footing with them as to borrow large sums of money from them. Do you object to this?"

"No," I said frankly, "I do not."

"Good! You will also mingle freely in Ambassadorial and foreign circles. It would be well for you to dine, at least once a week, with the British Ambassador. And now one final word" – here von Gestern spoke with singular impressiveness – "as to the President of the United States."

"Yes," I said.

"You must mix with him on a footing of the most open-handed friendliness. Be at the White House continually. Make yourself in the fullest sense of the words the friend and adviser of the President. All this I think is clear. In fact, it is only what is done, as you know, by all the masters of international diplomacy."

"Precisely," I said.

"Very good. And then," continued the Baron, "as soon as you find yourself sufficiently *en rapport* with everybody – or I should say," he added in correction, for the Baron shares fully in the present German horror of imported French words, "when you find yourself sufficiently in enggeknüpfter-verwandtschaft with everybody, you may then proceed to advance your peace terms. And now, my dear fellow," said the Baron, with a touch of genuine cordiality, "one word more. Are you in need of money?"

"Yes," I said.

"I thought so. But you will find that you need it less and less as you go on. Meantime, good-bye, and best wishes for your mission."

Such was, such is, in fact, the mission with which I am

accredited. I regard it as by far the most important mission with which I have been accredited by the Wilhelmstrasse. Yet I am compelled to admit that up to the present it has proved unsuccessful. My attempts to carry it out have been baffled. There is something perhaps in the atmosphere of this republic which obstructs the working of high diplomacy. For over five months now I have been waiting and willing to dine with the American Cabinet. They have not invited me. For four weeks I sat each night waiting in the J. hotel in Washington with my suit on ready to be asked. They did not come near me.

Nor have I yet received an intimation from the British Embassy inviting me to an informal lunch or to midnight supper with the Ambassador. Everybody who knows anything of the inside working of the international spy system will realize that without these invitations one can do nothing. Nor has the President of the United States given any sign. I have sent word to him, in cipher, that I am ready to dine with him on any day that may be convenient to both of us. He has made no move in the matter.

Under these circumstances an intrigue with any of the leaders of fashionable society has proved impossible. My attempts to approach them have been misunderstood – in fact, have led to my being invited to leave the J. hotel. The fact that I was compelled to leave it, owing to reasons that I cannot reveal, without paying my account, has occasioned unnecessary and dangerous comment. I connect it, in fact, with the singular attitude adopted by the B. hotel on my arrival in New York, to which I have already referred.

I have therefore been compelled to fall back on revelations and disclosures. Here again I find the American atmosphere singularly uncongenial. I have offered to reveal to the Secretary of State the entire family history of Ferdinand of Bulgaria for fifty dollars. He says it is not worth it. I have offered to the British Embassy the inside story of the Abdication of Constantine for five dollars. They say they know it and knew it before it happened. I have offered, for little more than a nominal sum, to blacken the character of every reigning family in Germany. I am told that it is not necessary.

Meantime, as it is impossible to return to Central Europe, I expect to open either a fruit store or a peanut stand very shortly in this great metropolis. I imagine that many of my former colleagues will soon be doing the same!

(1918)

Personal Adventures

in the Spirit World

I DO NOT write what follows with the expectation of convincing or converting anybody. We Spiritualists – or Spiritists (we call ourselves both, or either) – never ask anybody to believe us. If they do, well and good. If not, all right. Our attitude simply is that facts are facts. There they are; believe them or not as you like. As I said the other night, in conversation with Aristotle and John Bunyan and George Washington and a few others, why should anybody believe us? Aristotle, I recollect, said that all that he wished was that everybody should know how happy he was; and Washington said that for his part, if people only knew how bright and beautiful it all was where he was, they would willingly, indeed gladly, pay the mere dollar – itself only a nominal fee – that it cost to talk to him. Bunyan, I remember, added that he himself was quite happy.

But, as I say, I never ask anybody to believe me; the more so as I was once an absolute sceptic myself. As I see it now, I was prejudiced. The mere fact that spiritual *séances* and the services of a medium involved the payment of money condemned the whole thing in my eyes. I did not realise, as I do now, that these *medii*, like anybody else, have got to live; otherwise they would die and become spirits.

Nor would I now place these disclosures before the public

were it not that I think that in the present crisis they will prove of value to the Allied cause.

But let me begin at the beginning. My own conversion to spiritualism came about, like that of so many others, through the more-or-less casual remark of a Friend.

Noticing me one day gloomy and depressed, this Friend remarked to me: "Have you any belief in Spiritualism?" Had it come from any one else, I should have turned the question aside with a sneer.

But it so happens that I owe a great deal of gratitude to this particular Friend. It was he who, at a time when I was so afflicted with rheumatism that I could scarcely leap five feet into the air without pain, said to me one day quite casually: "Have you ever tried Pyro for your rheumatism?" One month later I could leap ten feet in the air (had I been able to) without the slightest malaise. The same man, I may add, hearing me one day exclaiming to myself: "Oh! If there were anything that would remove the stains from my clothes!" said to me very simply and quietly: "Have you ever washed them in Luxo?" It was he too who, noticing a haggard look on my face after breakfast one morning, inquired immediately what I had been eating for breakfast; after which, with a simplicity and directness which I shall never forget, he said: "Why not eat Humpo?"

Nor can I ever forget my feeling on another occasion when, hearing me exclaim aloud: "Oh! If there were only something invented for removing the proteins and amygdaloids from a carbonised diet and leaving only the pure nitrogenous life-giving elements!" seized my hand in his, and said in a voice thrilled with emotion: "There is! It has!"

The reader will understand, therefore, that a question, or query, from such a Friend was not to be put lightly aside. When he asked: "Do you believe in Spiritualism?" I answered with perfect courtesy: "To be quite frank, I do not."

There was silence between us for a time, and then my Friend said: "Have you ever given it a trial?"

I paused a moment, as the idea was a novel one.

"No," I answered, "to be quite candid, I have not."

Neither of us spoke for perhaps twenty minutes after this, when my Friend said: "Have you anything against it?"

I thought awhile and then: "Yes," I said, "I have."

My Friend remained silent for perhaps half an hour. Then he asked: "What?" I meditated for some time. Then I said:

"This – it seems to me that the whole thing is done for money. How utterly unnatural it is to call up the dead – one's great-grandfather, let us say – and pay money for talking to him."

"Precisely," said my Friend without a moment's pause. "I thought so. Now suppose I could bring you into contact with the spirit world through a medium, or through different *medii*, without there being any question of money, other than a merely nominal fee – the money being, as it were, left out of count, and regarded as only, so to speak, nominal, something given merely *pro forma* and *ad interim*. Under these circumstances, will you try the experiment?"

I rose and took my Friend's hand.

"My dear fellow," I said, "I not only will, but I shall."

From this conversation dated my connection with Spiritualism, which has since opened for me a new world.

It would be out of place for me to indicate the particular address or the particular methods employed by the agency to which my Friend introduced me. I am anxious to avoid anything approaching a commercial tinge in what I write. Moreover, their advertisement can be seen along with many others – all, I am sure, just as honourable and just as trustworthy – in the columns of any daily newspaper. As everybody knows, many methods are employed. The tapping of a table, the movement of a ouija board, or the voice of a trance medium, are only a few among the many devices by which the spirits now enter into communication with us. But in my own case the method used was not only simplicity itself, but was so framed as to carry with it the proof of its own genuineness. One had merely to speak into the receiver of a telephone, and the voice of the spirit was heard through the transmitter as in an ordinary telephone conversation.

It was only natural, after the scoffing remark that I had made, that I should begin with my great-grandfather. Nor can I ever forget the peculiar thrill that went through me when I was informed by the head of the agency that a tracer was being sent out for Great-grandfather to call him to the 'phone.

Great-grandfather – let me do him this justice – was prompt. He was there in three minutes. Whatever his line of business was in the spirit world – and I was never able to learn it – he must have left it immediately and hurried to the telephone. Whatever later dissatisfaction I may have had with Great-grandfather, let me state it fairly and honestly, he is at least a punctual man. Every time I called he came right away without delay. Let those who are inclined to cavil at the methods of the Spiritualists reflect how impossible it would be to secure such punctuality on anything but a basis of absolute honesty.

In my first conversation with Great-grandfather I found myself so absurdly nervous at the thought of the vast gulf of space and time across which we were speaking that I perhaps framed my questions somewhat too crudely.

"How are you, Great-grandfather?" I asked.

His voice came back to me as distinctly as if he were in the next room:

"I am happy, very happy. Please tell everybody that I am *happy*."

"Great-grandfather," I said, "I will. I'll see that everybody knows it. Where are you, Great-grandfather?"

"Here," he answered, "beyond."

"Beyond what?"

"Here on the other side."

"Side of which?" I asked.

"Of the great vastness," he answered. "The other end of the Illimitable."

"Oh, I see," I said, "that's where you are." We were silent for some time. It is amazing how difficult it is to find things to talk about with one's great-grandfather. For the life of me I could think of nothing better than: "What sort of weather have you been having?"

"There is no weather here," said Great-grandfather. "It's all bright and beautiful all the time."

"You mean bright sunshine?" I said.

"There is no sun here," said Great-grandfather.

"Then how do you mean —" I began.

But at this moment the head of the agency tapped me on the shoulder to remind me that the two minutes' conversation for which I had deposited, as a nominal fee, five dollars, had expired. The agency was courteous enough to inform me that for five dollars more Great-grandfather would talk another two minutes.

But I thought it preferable to stop for the moment.

Now I do not wish to say a word against my own great-grandfather. Yet in the conversations which followed on successive days I found him – how shall I put it? – unsatisfactory. He had been, when on this side – to use the term which we Spiritualists prefer – a singularly able man – an English judge; so at least I have always been given to understand. But somehow Great-grandfather's brain, on the other side, seemed to have got badly damaged. My own theory is that, living always in the bright sunshine, he had got sunstroke. But I may wrong him. Perhaps it was locomotor ataxia that he had. That he was very, very happy where he was is beyond all doubt. He said so at every conversation. But I have noticed that feeble-minded people are often happy. He said, too, that he was glad to be where he was; and on the whole I felt glad that he was too. Once or twice I thought that possibly Great-grandfather felt so happy because he had been drinking: his voice, even across the great gulf, seemed somehow to suggest it. But on being questioned he told me that where he was there was no drink and no thirst, because it was all so bright and beautiful. I asked him if he meant that it was "bone-dry" like Kansas, or whether the rich could still get it? But he didn't answer.

Our intercourse ended in a quarrel. No doubt it was my fault. But it *did* seem to me that Great-grandfather, who had been one of the greatest English lawyers of his day, might have handed out an opinion.

The matter came up thus: I had had an argument – it was in the middle of last winter – with some men at my club about the legal interpretation of the Adamson Law. The dispute grew bitter. "I'm right," I said, "and I'll prove it if you give me time to consult the authorities."

"Consult your great-grandfather!" sneered one of the men.

"All right," I said, "I will."

I walked straight across the room to the telephone and called up the agency. "Give me my great-grandfather," I said. "I want him right away."

He was there. Good, punctual old soul, I'll say that for him. He was there.

"Great-grandfather," I said, "I'm in a discussion here about the constitutionality of the Adamson Law, involving the power of Congress under the Constitution. Now, you remember the Constitution when they made it. Is the law all right?"

There was silence.

"How does it stand, Great-grandfather?" I said. "Will it hold water?"

Then he spoke.

"Over here," he said, "there are no laws, no members of Congress and no Adamsons; it's all bright and beautiful and —"

"Great-grandfather," I said, as I hung up the receiver in disgust, "you are a Mutt!" I never spoke to him again.

Yet I feel sorry for him, feeble old soul, flitting about in the Illimitable, and always so punctual to hurry to the telephone – so happy, so feeble-witted and so courteous; a better man, perhaps, take it all in all, than he was in life: lonely, too, it may be, out there in the Vastness. Yet I never called him up again. He is happy. Let him stay.

Indeed, my acquaintance with the spirit world might have ended at that point but for the good offices, once more, of my Friend.

"You find your great-grandfather a little slow, a little dull?" he said. "Well, then, if you want brains, power, energy, why not call up some of the spirits of the great men, some of the leading men, for instance, of your great-grandfather's time?"

"You've said it!" I exclaimed. "I'll call up Napoleon Bonaparte."

I hurried to the Agency.

"Is it possible," I asked, "for me to call up the Emperor Napoleon and talk to him?"

Possible? Certainly. It appeared that nothing was easier. In the case of Napoleon Bonaparte the nominal fee had to be ten dollars in place of five; but it seemed to me that if Great-grandfather cost five, Napoleon Bonaparte at ten was cheapness itself.

"Will it take long to get him?" I asked anxiously.

"We'll send out a tracer for him right away," they said.

Like Great-grandfather, Napoleon was punctual. That I will say for him. If in any way I think less of Napoleon Bonaparte now than I did, let me at least admit that a more punctual, obliging, willing man I never talked with.

He came in two minutes. "He's on the line now," they said. I took up the receiver, trembling.

"Hello!" I called. "*Est-ce que c'est l'Empereur Napoléon à qui j'ai l'honneur de parler?*"

"How's that?" said Napoleon.

"*Je demand si je suis en communication avec l'Empereur Napoléon —*"

"Oh!" said Napoleon, "that's all right; speak English."

"What!" I said in surprise. "You know English? I always thought you couldn't speak a word of it."

He was silent for a minute. Then he said:

"I picked it up over here. It's all right. Go right ahead."

"Well," I continued, "I've always admired you so much, your wonderful brain and genius, that I felt I wanted to speak to you and ask you how you are."

"Happy," said Napoleon, "very happy."

"That's good," I said, "that's fine! And how is it out there? All bright and beautiful, eh?"

"Very beautiful," said the Emperor.

"And just where are you," I continued. "Somewhere out in the Unspeakable, I suppose, eh?"

"Yes," he answered, "out here beyond."

"That's good," I said, "pretty happy, eh?"

"Very happy," said Napoleon. "Tell everybody how happy I am."

"I know," I answered, "I'll tell them all. But just now I've a particular thing to ask. We've got a big war on, pretty well the whole world in it, and I thought perhaps a few pointers from a man like you —"

But at this point the attendant touched me on the shoulder. "Your time is up," he said.

I was about to offer to pay at once for two minutes more when a better idea struck me. Talk with Napoleon? I'd do better than that. I'd call a whole War Council of great spirits, lay the war crisis before them and get the biggest brains that the world ever produced to work on how to win the war.

Whom should I have? Let me see! Napoleon himself,

of course. I'd bring him back. And for the sea business, the submarine problem, I'd have Admiral Nelson. George Washington, naturally, for the American end; for politics, say, good old Ben Franklin, the wisest old head that ever walked on American legs, and witty, too; yes, Franklin certainly, if only for his wit to keep the council from getting gloomy; Lincoln – honest old Abe – him certainly I must have. Those and perhaps a few others.

I reckoned that a consultation at ten dollars apiece with spirits of that class was cheap to the verge of the ludicrous. Their advice ought to be worth millions – yes, billions – to the cause.

The agency got them for me without trouble. There is no doubt they are a punctual crowd, over there beyond in the Unthinkable.

I gathered them all in and talked to them, all and severally, the payment, a merely nominal matter, being made, *pro forma*, in advance.

I have in front of me in my rough notes the result of their advice. When properly drafted it will be, I feel sure, one of the most important state documents produced in the war.

In the personal sense – I have to admit it – I found them just a trifle disappointing. Franklin, poor fellow, has apparently lost his wit. The spirit of Lincoln seemed to me to have none of that homely wisdom that he used to have. And it appears that we were quite mistaken in thinking Benjamin Disraeli a brilliant man; it is clear to me now that he was dull – just about as dull as Great-grandfather, I should say. Washington, too, is not at all the kind of man we thought him.

Still, these are only personal impressions. They detract nothing from the extraordinary value of the advice given, which seems to me to settle once and forever any lingering doubt about the value of communications with the Other Side.

My draft of their advice runs in part as follows:

The Spirit of Admiral Nelson, on being questioned on the submarine problem, holds that if all the men on the submarines were where he is everything would be bright and happy. This seems to me an invaluable hint. There is nothing needed now except to put them there.

The advice of the Spirit of Napoleon about the campaign on land seemed to me, if possible, of lower value than that of Nelson on the campaign at sea. It is hardly conceivable that Napoleon has forgotten where the Marne is. But it may have changed since his day. At any rate, he says that if ever the Russians cross the Marne, all is over. Coming from such a master-strategist, this ought to be attended to.

Franklin, on being asked whether the United States had done right in going into the war, said Yes; asked whether the country could with honour have stayed out, he said No. There is guidance here for thinking men of all ranks.

Lincoln is very happy where he is. So too, I was amazed to find, is Disraeli. In fact, it was most gratifying to learn that all of the great spirits consulted are very happy, and want everybody to know how happy they are. Where they are, I may say, it is all bright and beautiful.

Fear of trespassing on their time prevented me from questioning each of them up to the full limit of the period contracted for.

I understand that I have still to my credit at the agency five minutes' talk with Napoleon, available at any time, and similarly five minutes each with Franklin and Washington, to say nothing of ten minutes' unexpired time with Great-grandfather.

All of these opportunities I am willing to dispose of at a reduced rate to any one still sceptical of the reality of the spirit world.

(1918)

War and Peace

at the Galaxy Club

THE GREAT Peace Kermesse at the Galaxy Club, to which I have the honour to belong, held with a view to wipe out the Peace Deficit of the Club, has just ended. For three weeks our club house has been a blaze of illumination. We have had four orchestras in attendance. There have been suppers and dances every night. Our members have not spared themselves.

The Kermesse is now over. We have time, as our lady members are saying, to turn round.

For the moment we are sitting listening, amid bursts of applause, to our treasurer's statement. As we hear it we realise that this Peace Kermesse has proved the culmination and crown of four winters' war work.

But I must explain from the beginning.

Our efforts began with the very opening of the war. We felt that a rich organisation like ours ought to do something for the relief of the Belgians. At the same time we felt that our members would rather receive something in the way of entertainment for their money than give it straight out of their pockets.

We therefore decided first to hold a public lecture in the club, and engaged the services of Professor Dry to lecture on the causes of the war.

In view of the circumstances, Professor Dry very kindly reduced his lecture fee, which (he assured us) is generally two hundred and fifty dollars, to two hundred and forty.

The lecture was most interesting. Professor Dry traced the causes of the War backwards through the Middle Ages. He showed that it represented the conflict of the brachiocephalic culture of the Wendic races with the dolichocephalic culture of the Alpine stock. At the time when the lights went out he had got it back to the eighth century before Christ.

Unfortunately the night, being extremely wet, was unfavourable. Few of our members care to turn out to lectures in wet weather. The treasurer was compelled to announce to the Committee a net deficit of two hundred dollars. Some of the ladies of the Committee moved that the entire deficit be sent to the Belgians, but were overruled by the interference of the men.

But the error was seen to have been in the choice of the lecturer. Our members were no longer interested in the *causes* of the war. The topic was too old. We therefore held another public lecture in the club, on the topic *What Will Come After the War.* It was given by a very talented gentleman, a Mr. Guess, a most interesting speaker, who reduced his fee (as the thing was a war charity) by one-half, leaving it at three hundred dollars. Unhappily the weather was against us. It was too fine. Our members scarcely care to listen to lectures in fine weather. And it turned out that our members are not interested in what will come after the war. The topic is too new. Our receipts of fifty dollars left us with a net deficit of two hundred and fifty. Our treasurer therefore proposed that we should carry both deficits forward and open a Special Patriotic Entertainment Account showing a net total deficit of four hundred and fifty dollars.

In the opinion of the committee our mistake had been in engaging outside talent. It was felt that the cost of this was prohibitive. It was better to invite the services of the members of the club themselves. A great number of the ladies expressed their willingness to take part in any kind of war work that took the form of public entertainment.

Accordingly we presented a play. It was given in the ball room of the club house, a stage being specially put up for us by a firm of contractors. The firm (as a matter of patriotism) did the whole thing for us at cost, merely charging us with the labour, the material, the time, the thought and the anxiety that they gave to the job, but for nothing else. In fact, the whole staging, including lights, plumbing and decorations was merely a matter of five hundred dollars. The plumbers very considerately made no charge for their time, but only for their work.

It was felt that it would be better to have a new play than an old. We selected a brilliant little modern drawing-room comedy never yet presented. The owner of the copyright, a theatrical firm, let us use it for a merely nominal fee of two hundred dollars, including the sole right to play the piece forever. There being only twenty-eight characters in it, it was felt to be more suitable than a more ambitious thing. The tickets were placed at one dollar, no one being admitted free except the performers themselves, and the members who very kindly acted as scene shifters, curtain lifters, ushers, doorkeepers, programme sellers, and the general committee of management. All the performers, at their own suggestion, supplied their own costumes, charging nothing to the club except the material and the cost of dressmaking. Beyond this there was no expense except for the fee, very reasonable, of Mr. Skip, the professional coach who trained the performers, and who asked us, in view of the circumstances, less than half of what he would have been willing to accept.

The proceeds were to be divided between the Belgian Fund and the Red Cross, giving fifty per cent to each. A motion in amendment from the ladies' financial committee to give fifty per cent to the Belgian Fund and sixty per cent to the Red Cross was voted down.

Unfortunately it turned out that the idea of a *play* was a mistake in judgment. Our members, it seemed, did not care to go to see a play except in a theatre. A great number of them, however, very kindly turned out to help in shifting the scenery and in acting as ushers.

Our treasurer announced, as the result of the play, a net deficit of twelve hundred dollars. He moved, with general applause, that it be carried forward.

The total deficit having now reached over sixteen hundred dollars, there was a general feeling that a very special effort must be made to remove it. It was decided to hold Weekly Patriotic Dances in the club ball room, every Saturday evening. No charge was made for admission to the dances, but a War Supper was served at one dollar a head.

Unfortunately the dances, as first planned, proved again an error. It appeared that though our members are passionately fond of dancing, few if any of them cared to eat at night. The plan was therefore changed. The supper was served first, and was free, and for the dancing after supper a charge was made of one dollar per person. This again was an error. It seems that after our members have had supper they prefer to go home and sleep. After one winter of dancing the treasurer announced a total Patriotic Relief Deficit of five thousand dollars, to be carried forward to next year. This sum duly appeared in the annual balance sheet of the club. The members, especially the ladies, were glad to think that we were at least doing *something* for the war.

At this point some of our larger men, themselves financial experts, took hold. They said that our entertainments had been on too small a scale. They told us that we had been "undermined by overhead expenses." The word "overhead" was soon on everybody's lips. We were told that if we could "distribute our overhead" it would disappear. It was therefore planned to hold a great War Kermesse with a view to spreading out the overhead so thin that it would vanish.

But it was at this very moment that the Armistice burst upon us in a perfectly unexpected fashion. Everyone of our members was, undoubtedly, delighted that the war was over but there was a very general feeling that it would have been better if we could have had a rather longer notice of what was coming. It seemed, as many of our members said, such a leap in the dark to rush into peace all at once. It was said indeed by our best business men that in financial circles they had been fully aware that there was a danger of peace for some time and had taken steps to discount the peace risk.

But for the club itself the thing came with a perfect crash. The whole preparation of the great Kermesse was well under way when the news broke upon us. For a time the members were aghast. It looked like ruin. But presently it was suggested that it might still be possible to save the club by turning the whole affair into a Peace Kermesse and devoting the proceeds to some suitable form of relief. Luckily it was discovered that there was still a lot of starvation in Russia, and fortunately it turned out that in spite of the armistice the Turks were still killing the Armenians.

So it was decided to hold the Kermesse and give all the profits realised by it to the Victims of the Peace. Everybody set to work again with a will. The Kermesse indeed had to be postponed for a few months to make room for the changes needed, but it has now been held and, in a certain sense, it has been the wildest kind of success. The club, as I said, has been a blaze of light for three weeks. We have had four orchestras in attendance every evening. There have been booths draped with the flags of all the Allies, except some that we were not sure about, in every corridor of the club. There have been dinner parties and dances every evening. The members, especially the ladies, have not spared themselves. Many of them have spent practically all their time at the Kermesse, not getting home until two in the morning.

And yet somehow one has felt that underneath the surface it was not a success. The spirit seemed gone out of it. The members themselves confessed in confidence that in spite of all they could do their hearts were not in it. Peace had somehow taken away all the old glad sense of enjoyment. As to spending money at the Kermesse all the members admitted frankly that they had no heart for it. This was especially the case when the rumour got abroad that the Armenians were a poor lot and that some of the Turks were quite gentlemanly fellows. It was said, too, that if the Russians did starve it would do them a lot of good.

So it was known even before we went to hear the financial report that there would be no question of profits on the Kermesse going to the Armenians or the Russians.

And to-night the treasurer has been reading out to a general meeting the financial results as nearly as they can be computed.

He has put the Net Patriotic Deficit, as nearly as he can estimate it, at fifteen thousand dollars, though he has stated, with applause from the ladies, that the Gross Deficit is bigger still.

The Ladies Financial Committee has just carried a motion that the whole of the deficit, both net and gross, be now forwarded to the Red Cross Society (sixty per cent), the Belgian Relief Fund (fifty per cent), and the remainder invested in the War Loan.

But there is a very general feeling among the male members that the club will have to go into liquidation. Peace has ruined us. Not a single member, so far as I am aware, is prepared to protest against the peace, or is anything but delighted to think that the war is over. At the same time we *do* feel that if

ve could have had a longer notice, six months for instance, we
ould have braced ourselves better to stand up against it and
meet the blow when it fell.

I think, too, that our feeling is shared outside.

(1919)

Buggam Grange:

A Good Old Ghost Story

THE EVENING was already falling as the vehicle in which was contained entered upon the long and gloomy avenu that leads to Buggam Grange.

A resounding shriek echoed through the wood as I entered the avenue. I paid no attention to it at the moment, judging to be merely one of those resounding shrieks which one migh expect to hear in such a place at such a time. As my drive continued, however, I found myself wondering in spite of mysel why such a shriek should have been uttered at the very moment of my approach.

I am not by temperament in any degree a nervous man and yet there was much in my surroundings to justify a certain feeling of apprehension. The Grange is situated in the loneliest part of England, the marsh country of the fens to which civilization has still hardly penetrated. The inhabitants, of whom there are only one and a half to the square mile, live here and there among the fens and eke out a miserable existence by frog fishing and catching flies. They speak a dialect so broken as to be practically unintelligible, while the perpetual rain which falls upon them renders speech itself almost superfluous.

Here and there where the ground rises slightly above the level of the fens there are dense woods tangled with parasitic creepers and filled with owls. Bats fly from wood to wood. The air on the lower ground is charged with the poisonous gases which exude from the marsh, while in the woods it is heavy with the dank odours of deadly nightshade and poison ivy.

It had been raining in the afternoon, and as I drove up the avenue the mournful dripping of the rain from the dark trees accentuated the cheerlessness of the gloom. The vehicle in which I rode was a fly on three wheels, the fourth having apparently been broken and taken off, causing the fly to sag on one side and drag on its axle over the muddy ground, the fly thus moving only at a foot's pace in a way calculated to enhance the dreariness of the occasion. The driver on the box in front of me was so thickly muffled up as to be indistinguishable, while the horse which drew us was so thickly coated with mist as to be practically invisible. Seldom, I may say, have I had a drive of so mournful a character.

The avenue presently opened out upon a lawn with overgrown shrubberies and in the half darkness I could see the outline of the Grange itself, a rambling, dilapidated building. A dim light struggled through the casement of a window in a tower room. Save for the melancholy cry of a row of owls sitting on the roof, and croaking of the frogs in the moat which ran around the grounds, the place was soundless. My driver halted his horse at the hither side of the moat. I tried in vain to urge him, by signs, to go further. I could see by the fellow's face that he was in a paroxysm of fear and indeed nothing but the extra sixpence which I had added to his fare would have made him undertake the drive up the avenue. I had no sooner alighted than he wheeled his cab about and made off.

Laughing heartily at the fellow's trepidation (I have a way of laughing heartily in the dark), I made my way to the door and pulled the bell-handle. I could hear the muffled reverberations of the bell far within the building. Then all was silent. I bent my ear to listen, but could hear nothing except perhaps the sound of a low moaning as of a person in pain or in great mental distress. Convinced, however, from what my friend Sir Jeremy Buggam had told me, that the Grange was not empty, I raised the ponderous knocker and beat with it loudly against the door.

But perhaps at this point I may do well to explain to my readers (before they are too frightened to listen to me) how I came to be beating on the door of Buggam Grange at nightfall on a gloomy November evening.

A year before I had been sitting with Sir Jeremy Buggam, the present baronet, on the verandah of his ranch in California.

"So you don't believe in the supernatural?" he was saying.

"Not in the slightest," I answered, lighting a cigar as I spoke. When I want to speak very positively, I generally light a cigar as I speak.

"Well, at any rate, Digby," said Sir Jeremy, "Buggam Grange is haunted. If you want to be assured of it go down there any time and spend the night and you'll see for yourself."

"My dear fellow," I replied, "nothing will give me greater pleasure. I shall be back in England in six weeks, and I shall be delighted to put your ideas to the test. Now tell me," I added somewhat cynically, "is there any particular season or day when your Grange is supposed to be specially terrible?"

Sir Jeremy looked at me strangely. "Why do you ask that?" he said. "Have you heard the story of the Grange?"

"Never heard of the place in my life," I answered cheerily, "till you mentioned it to-night, my dear fellow, I hadn't the remotest idea that you still owned property in England."

"The Grange is shut up," said Sir Jeremy, "and has been for twenty years. But I keep a man there – Horrod – he was butler in my father's time and before. If you care to go, I'll write him that you're coming. And since you are taking your own fate in your hands, the fifteenth of November is the day."

At that moment Lady Buggam and Clara and the other girls came trooping out on the verandah, and the whole thing passed clean out of my mind. Nor did I think of it again until I was back in London. Then by one of those strange coincidences or premonitions – call it what you will – it suddenly occurred to me one morning that it was the fifteenth of November. Whether Sir Jeremy had written to Horrod or not, I did not know. But none the less nightfall found me, as I have described, knocking at the door of Buggam Grange.

The sound of the knocker had scarcely ceased to echo when I heard the shuffling of feet within, and the sound of chains and bolts being withdrawn. The door opened. A man stood before me holding a lighted candle which he shaded with his hand. His faded black clothes, once apparently a butler's dress, his white hair and advanced age left me in no doubt that he was Horrod of whom Sir Jeremy had spoken.

Without a word he motioned me to come in, and, still without speech, he helped me to remove my wet outer garments, and then beckoned me into a great room, evidently the dining room of the Grange.

I am not in any degree a nervous man by temperament, as I think I remarked before, and yet there was something in the vastness of the wainscotted room, lighted only by a single candle, and in the silence of the empty house, and still more in the appearance of my speechless attendant which gave me a feeling of distinct uneasiness. As Horrod moved to and fro I took occasion to scrutinize his face more narrowly. I have seldom seen features more calculated to inspire a nervous dread. The pallor of his face and the whiteness of his hair (the man was at least seventy), and still more the peculiar furtiveness of his eyes, seemed to mark him as one who lived under a great terror. He moved with a noiseless step and at times he turned his head to glance in the dark corners of the room.

"Sir Jeremy told me," I said, speaking as loudly and as heartily as I could, "that he would apprise you of my coming."

I was looking into his face as I spoke.

In answer Horrod laid his finger across his lips and I knew

that he was deaf and dumb. I am not nervous (I think I said that), but the realization that my sole companion in the empty house was a deaf mute struck a cold chill to my heart.

Horrod laid in front of me a cold meat pie, a cold goose, a cheese, and a tall flagon of cider. But my appetite was gone. I ate the goose, but found that after I had finished the pie I had but little zest for the cheese, which I finished without enjoyment. The cider had a sour taste, and after having permitted Horrod to refill the flagon twice, I found that it induced a sense of melancholy and decided to drink no more.

My meal finished, the butler picked up the candle and beckoned to me to follow him. We passed through the empty corridors of the house, a long line of pictured Buggams looking upon us as we passed, their portraits in the flickering light of the taper assuming a strange and life-like appearance as if leaning forward from their frames to gaze upon the intruder.

Horrod led me upstairs and I realized that he was taking me to the tower in the east wing in which I had observed a light.

The rooms to which the butler conducted me consisted of a sitting room with an adjoining bedroom, both of them fitted with antique wainscotting against which a faded tapestry fluttered. There was a candle burning on the table in the sitting room but its insufficient light only rendered the surroundings the more dismal. Horrod bent down in front of the fireplace and endeavoured to light a fire there. But the wood was evidently damp, and the fire flickered feebly on the hearth.

The butler left me, and in the stillness of the house I could hear his shuffling step echo down the corridor. It may have been fancy, but it seemed to me that his departure was the signal for a low moan that came from somewhere behind the wainscot. There was a narrow cupboard door at one side of the room, and for the moment I wondered whether the moaning came from within. I am not as a rule lacking in courage (I am sure my reader will be decent enough to believe this), yet I found myself entirely unwilling to open the cupboard door and look within. In place of doing so I seated myself in a great chair in front of the feeble fire. I must have been seated there for some time when I happened to lift my eyes to the mantel above and saw, standing upon it, a letter addressed to myself. I knew the handwriting at once to be that of Sir Jeremy Buggam.

I opened it, and spreading it out within reach of the feeble candle light, I read as follows:

"*My dear Digby,*

In our talk that you will remember I had no time to finish telling you about the mystery of Buggam Grange. I take for granted, however, that you will go there and that Horrod will put you in the tower rooms, which are the only ones that make any pretense of being habitable. I have, therefore, sent him this letter to deliver at the Grange itself. The story is this:

On the night of the fifteenth of November, fifty years ago, my grandfather was murdered in the room in which you are sitting, by his cousin Sir Duggam Buggam. He was stabbed from behind while seated at the little table at which you are probably reading this letter. The two had been playing cards at the table and my grandfather's body was found lying in a litter of cards and gold sovereigns on the floor. Sir Duggam Buggam, insensible from drink, lay beside him, the fatal knife at his hand, his fingers smeared with blood. My grandfather, though of the younger branch, possessed a part of the estates which were to revert to Sir Duggam on his death. Sir Duggam Buggam was tried at the Assizes and was hanged. On the day of his execution he was permitted by the authorities, out of respect for his rank, to wear a mask to the scaffold. The clothes in which he was executed are hanging at full length in the little cupboard to your right, and the mask is above them. It is said that on every fifteenth of November at midnight the cupboard door opens and Sir Duggam Buggam walks out into the room. It has been found impossible to get servants to remain at the

Grange, and the place – except for the presence of Horrod – has been unoccupied for a generation. At the time of the murder Horrod was a young man of twenty-two, newly entered into the service of the family. It was he who entered the room and discovered the crime. On the day of the execution he was stricken with paralysis and has never spoken since. From that time to this he has never consented to leave the Grange where he lives in isolation.

Wishing you a pleasant night after your tiring journey,

I remain,

Very faithfully,

JEREMY BUGGAM."

I leave my reader to imagine my state of mind when I completed the perusal of the letter.

I have as little belief in the supernatural as any one, yet I must confess that there was something in the surroundings in which I now found myself which rendered me at least uncomfortable. My reader may smile if he will, but I assure him that it was with a very distinct feeling of uneasiness that I at length managed to rise to my feet, and, grasping my candle in my hand, to move backward into the bedroom. As I backed into it something so like a moan seemed to proceed from the closed cupboard that I accelerated my backward movement to a considerable degree. I hastily blew out the candle, threw myself upon the bed and drew the bed clothes over my head, keeping, however, one eye and one ear still out and available.

How long I lay thus listening to every sound, I cannot tell. The stillness had become absolute. From time to time I could dimly hear the distant cry of an owl and once far away in the building below a sound as of some one dragging a chain along a floor. More than once I was certain that I heard the sound of moaning behind the wainscot. Meantime I realized that the hour must now be drawing close upon the fatal moment of midnight. My watch I could not see in the darkness, but by reckoning the time that must have elapsed I knew that midnight could not be far away. Then presently my ear, alert to every sound, could just distinguish far away across the fens the striking of a church bell, in the clock tower of Buggam village church, no doubt, tolling the hour of twelve.

On the last stroke of twelve, the cupboard door in the next room opened. There is no need to ask me how I knew it. I couldn't, of course, see it, but I could hear, or sense in some way, the sound of it. I could feel my hair, all of it, rising upon my head. I was aware that there was a *presence* in the adjoining room, I will not say a person, a living soul, but a *presence*. Any one who has been in the next room to a presence will know just how I felt. I could hear a sound as of some one groping on the floor and the faint rattle as of coins.

My hair was now perpendicular. My reader can blame it or not, but it was.

Then at this very moment from somewhere below in the building there came the sound of a prolonged and piercing cry, a cry as of a soul passing in agony. My reader may censure me or not, but right at this moment I decided to beat it. Whether I should have remained to see what was happening is a question that I will not discuss. My one idea was to get out and to get out quickly. The window of the tower room was some twenty-five feet above the ground. I sprang out through the casement in one leap and landed on the grass below. I jumped over the shrubbery in one bound and cleared the moat in one jump. I went down the avenue in about six strides and ran five miles along the road through the fens in three minutes. This at least is an accurate transcription of my sensations. It may have taken longer. I never stopped till I found myself on the threshold of the Buggam Arms in Little Buggam, beating on the door for the landlord.

I returned to Buggam Grange on the next day in the bright sunlight of a frosty November morning, in a seven cylinder motor car with six local constables and a physician. It makes all the difference. We carried revolvers, spades, pickaxes, shot-guns and a ouija board.

What we found cleared up forever the mystery of the Grange. We discovered Horrod the butler lying on the dining room floor quite dead. The physician said that he had died from heart failure. There was evidence from the marks of his shoes in the dust that he had come in the night to the tower room. On the table he had placed a paper which contained a full confession of his having murdered Jeremy Buggam fifty years before. The circumstances of the murder had rendered it easy for him to fasten the crime upon Sir Duggam, already insensible from drink. A few minutes with the ouija board enabled us to get a full corroboration from Sir Duggam. He promised moreover, now that his name was cleared, to go away from the premises forever.

My friend, the present Sir Jeremy, has rehabilitated Bug-gam Grange. The place is rebuilt. The moat is drained. The whole house is lit with electricity. There are beautiful motor drives in all directions in the woods. He has had the bats shot and the owls stuffed. His daughter, Clara Buggam, became my wife. She is looking over my shoulder as I write. What more do you want?

(1920)

How We Kept Mother's Day

As Related by a Member of the Family

O F ALL THE different ideas that have been started lately, I think that the very best is the notion of celebrating once a year "Mother's Day." I don't wonder that May the eleventh is becoming such a popular date all over America, and I am sure that the idea will spread to England too.

It is especially in a big family like ours that such an idea takes hold. So we decided to have a special celebration of Mother's birthday. We thought it a fine idea. It made us all realize how much Mother had done for us for years, and all the efforts and sacrifice that she had made for our sake.

So we decided that we'd make it a great day, a holiday for all the family, and do everything we could to make Mother happy. Father decided to take a holiday from his office, so as to help in celebrating the day, and my sister Anne and I stayed home from college classes, and Mary and my brother Will stayed home from High School.

It was our plan to make it a day just like Christmas or any big holiday, and so we decided to decorate the house with flowers and with mottoes over the mantelpieces, and all that kind of thing. We got Mother to make mottoes and arrange the decorations, because she always does it at Christmas.

The two girls thought it would be a nice thing to dress in our very best for such a big occasion, and so they both got new hats. Mother trimmed both the hats, and they looked fine, and Father had bought four-in-hand silk ties for himself and us boys as a souvenir of the day to remember Mother by. We were going to get Mother a new hat too, but it turned out that she seemed to really like her old grey bonnet better than a new one, and both the girls said that it was awfully becoming to her.

Well, after breakfast we had it arranged as a surprise for Mother that we would hire a motor-car and take her for a beautiful drive away into the country. Mother is hardly ever able to have a treat like that, because we can only afford to keep one maid, and so Mother is busy in the house nearly all the time. And of course the country is so lovely now that it would be just grand for her to have a lovely morning driving for miles and miles.

But on the very morning of the day we changed the plan a little bit, because it occurred to Father that a thing it would be better to do even than to take Mother for a motor drive would be to take her fishing. Father said that as the car was hired and paid for, we might just as well use it for a drive up into hills where the streams are. As Father said, if you just go out driving without any object, you have a sense of aimlessness, but if you are going to fish, there is definite purpose in front of you to heighten the enjoyment.

So we all felt that it would be nicer for Mother to have a definite purpose; and anyway, it turned out that Father had just got a new rod the day before, which made the idea of fishing all the more appropriate, and he said that Mother could use it if she wanted to, in fact, he said it was practically for her, only Mother said she would much rather watch him fish and not try to fish herself.

So we got everything arranged for the trip, and we got Mother to cut up some sandwiches and make up a sort of lunch in case we got hungry, though of course we were to come back home again to a big dinner in the middle of the day, just like Christmas or New Year's Day. Mother packed it all up in a basket for us ready to go in the motor.

Well, when the car came to the door, it turned out that there hardly seemed as much room in it as we had supposed, because we hadn't reckoned on Father's fishing basket and the rods and the lunch, and it was plain enough that we couldn't all get in.

Father said not to mind him; he said that he could just as well stay home, and that he was sure that he could put in the time working in the garden; he said that there was a lot of rough dirty work that he could do, like digging a trench for the garbage, that would save hiring a man, and so he said that he'd stay home; he said that we were not to let the fact of his not having had a real holiday for three years stand in our way; he wanted us to go right ahead and be happy and have a big day, and not to mind him. He said that he could plug away all day, and in fact he said he'd been a fool to think there'd be any holiday for him.

But of course we all felt that it would never do to let Father stay home, especially as we knew he would make trouble if he did. The two girls, Anne and Mary, would gladly have stayed and helped the maid get dinner, only it seemed such a pity to on a lovely day like this, having their new hats. But they both said that Mother had only to say the word, and they'd gladly stay home and work. Will and I would have dropped out, but unfortunately we wouldn't have been any use in getting the dinner.

So in the end it was decided that Mother would stay home and just have a lovely restful day round the house, and get the dinner. It turned out anyway that Mother doesn't care for fishing, and also it was just a little bit cold and fresh out of doors, though it was lovely and sunny, and Father was afraid that Mother might take cold if she came.

He said he would never forgive himself if he dragged Mother round the country and let her take a severe cold at a time when she might be having a beautiful rest. He said it was our duty to try and let Mother get all the rest and quiet that she could, after all that she had done for all of us, and he said that was principally why he had fallen in with the idea of a fishing trip, so as to give Mother a little quiet. He said that young people seldom realize how much quiet means to people who are getting old. As to himself, he could still stand the racket, but he was glad to shelter Mother from it.

So we all drove away with three cheers for Mother, and Mother stood and watched us from the veranda for as long as she could see us, and Father waved his hand back to her every few minutes till he hit his hand on the back edge of the car, and then said that he didn't think that Mother could see us any longer.

Well, – we had the loveliest day up among the hills that you could possibly imagine, and Father caught such big specimens that he felt sure that Mother couldn't have landed them anyway, if she had been fishing for them, and Will and I fished too, though we didn't get so many as Father, and the two girls met quite a lot of people that they knew as we drove along, and there were some young men friends of theirs that they met along the stream and talked to, and so we all had a splendid time.

It was quite late when we got back, nearly seven o'clock in the evening, but Mother had guessed that we would be late, so she had kept back the dinner so as to have it just nicely ready and hot for us. Only first she had to get towels and soap for Father and clean things for him to put on, because he always gets so messed up with fishing, and that kept Mother busy for a little while, that and helping the girls get ready.

But at last everything was ready, and we sat down to the grandest kind of dinner – roast turkey and all sorts of things like on Christmas Day. Mother had to get up and down a good bit during the meal fetching things back and forward, but at the end Father noticed it and he said she simply mustn't do it, that he wanted her to spare herself, and he got up and fetched the walnuts over from the sideboard himself.

The dinner lasted a long while, and was great fun, and when it was over all of us wanted to help clear the things up and wash the dishes, only Mother said that she would really much rather do it, and so we let her, because we wanted just for once to humour her.

It was quite late when it was all over, and when we all kissed Mother before going up to bed, she said it had been the most wonderful day in her life, and I think there were tears in her eyes. So we all felt awfully repaid for all that we had done.

(1926)

Old Junk and New Money

A Little Study in the Latest Antiques

I WENT THE other day into the beautiful home of my two good friends, the Hespeler-Hyphen-Joneses, and I paused a moment, as my eye fell on the tall clock that stood in the hall.

"Ah," said Hespeler-Hyphen-Jones, "I see you are looking at the clock – a beautiful thing, isn't it? – a genuine antique."

"Does it go?" I asked.

"Good gracious, no!" exclaimed my two friends. "But isn't it a beautiful thing!"

"Did it ever go?"

"I doubt it," said Hespeler-Hyphen-Jones. "The works, of course, are by Salvolatile – one of the really *great* clockmakers, you know. But I don't know whether the works ever went. That, I believe, is one way in which you can always tell a Salvolatile. If it's a genuine Salvolatile, it won't go."

"In any case," I said, "it has no hands."

"Oh, dear, no," said Mrs. Jones. "It never had, as far as we know. We picked it up in such a queer little shop in Amalfi and the man assured us that it never had had any hands. He guaranteed it. That's one of the things, you know, that you can tell by. Charles and I were terribly keen about clocks at that time and really studied them, and the books all agreed that no genuine Salvolatile has any hands."

"And was the side broken, too, when you got it," I asked.

"Ah, no," said my friend. "We had that done by an expert in New York after we got back. Isn't it exquisitely done? You see, he has made the break to look exactly as if some one had rolled the clock over and stamped on it. Every genuine Salvolatile is said to have been stamped upon like that.

"Of course, our break is only imitation, but it's extremely well done, isn't it? We go to Ferrugi's, that little place on Fourth Avenue, you know, for everything that we want broken. They have a splendid man there. He can break anything."

"Really!" I said.

"Yes, and the day when we wanted the clock done, Charles and I went down to see him do it. It was really quite wonderful, wasn't it, Charles?"

"Yes, indeed. The man laid the clock on the floor and turned it on its side and then stood looking at it intently, and walking round and round it and murmuring in Italian as if he were swearing at it. Then he jumped in the air and came down on it with both feet."

"Did he?" I asked.

"Yes, and with such wonderful accuracy. Our friend Mr. Appin-Hyphen-Smith – the great expert, you know – was looking at our clock last week and he said it was marvelous, hardly to be distinguished from a genuine *fractura*."

"But he did say, didn't he, dear," said Mrs. Jones, "that the better way is to throw a clock out of a fourth story window? You see, that was the height of the Italian houses in the Thirteenth Century – is it the Thirteenth Century I mean, Charles?"

"Yes," said Charles.

"Do you know, the other day I made the silliest mistake about a spoon. I thought it was a Twelfth Century spoon and said so and in reality it was only Eleven and a half. Wasn't it, Charles?"

"Yes," said Charles.

"But do come into the drawing room and have some tea.

And, by the way, since you are interested in antiques, do look please at my teapot."

"It looks an excellent teapot," I said, feeling it with my hand, "and it must have been very expensive, wasn't it?"

"Oh, not *that* one," interposed Mr. Hespeler-Hyphen-Jones. "That is nothing. We got that here in New York at Hoffany's – to make tea in. It *is* made of solid silver, of course, and all that, but even Hoffany's admitted that it was made in America and was probably not more than a year or so old and had never been used by anybody else. In fact, they couldn't guarantee it in any way."

"Oh, I see," I said.

"But let me pour you out tea from it and then do look at the perfect darling beside it. Oh, don't touch it, please, it won't stand up."

"Won't stand up?" I said.

"No," said Hespeler-Jones, "that's one of the tests. We know from that that it is genuine Swaatsmaacher. None of them stand up."

"Where did you buy it," I asked, "here?"

"Oh, heavens, no, you couldn't buy a thing like that here! As a matter of fact, we picked it up in a little gin shop in Obehellandam in Holland. Do you know Obehellandam?"

"I don't," I said.

"It's just the dearest little place, nothing but little wee smelly shops filled with most delightful things – all antique, everything broken. They guarantee that there is nothing in the shop that wasn't smashed at least a hundred years ago."

"You don't use the teapot to make tea," I said.

"Oh, no," said Mrs. Hespeler-Jones as she handed me a cup of tea from the New York teapot. "I don't think you could. It leaks."

"That again is a thing," said her husband, "that the experts always look for in a Swaatsmaacher. If it doesn't leak, it's probably just a faked-up thing not twenty years old."

"Is it silver?" I asked.

"Ah, no. That's another test," said Mrs. Jones. "The real Swaatsmaachers were always made of pewter bound with barrel-iron off the gin barrels. They try to imitate it now by using silver, but they can't get it."

"No, the silver won't take the tarnish," interjected her husband. "You see, it's the same way with ever so many of the old things. They rust and rot in a way that you simply cannot imitate. I have an old drinking horn that I'll show you presently – Ninth Century, isn't it, dear? – that is all coated inside with the most beautiful green slime, absolutely impossible to reproduce."

"Is it?" I said.

"Yes, I took it to Squeeziou's, the Italian place in London. (They are the great experts on horns, you know; they can tell exactly the century and the breed of cow.) And they told me that they had tried in vain to reproduce that peculiar and beautiful rot. One of their head men said that he thought that this horn had probably been taken from a dead cow that had been buried for fifty years. That's what gives it its value, you know."

"You didn't buy it in London, did you?" I asked.

"Oh, no," answered Hespeler-Jones. "London is perfectly impossible – just as hopeless as New York. You can't buy anything real there at all."

"Then where do you get all your things?" I asked, as I looked round at the collection of junk in the room.

"Oh, we pick them up here and there," said Mrs. Jones. "Just in any out-of-the-way corners. That little stool we found at the back of a cow stable in Loch Aberlocherty. They were actually using it for milking. And the two others – aren't they beautiful? though really it's quite wrong to have two chairs alike in the same room – came from the back of a tiny little whiskey shop in Galway. Such a delight of an old Irishman sold them to us and he admitted that he himself had no idea how old they were. They might, he said, be Fifteenth Century, or they might not.

"But, oh, Charles," my hostess interrupted herself to say, "I've just had a letter from Jane (Jane is my sister, you know) that is terribly exciting. She's found a table at a tiny place in Brittany that she thinks would exactly do in our card room. She says that it is utterly unlike anything else in the room and has quite obviously no connection with cards. But let me read what she says – let me see, yes, here's where it begins:

"'. . . a perfectly sweet little table. It probably had four legs originally and even now has two which, I am told, is a great find, as most people have to be content with one. The man explained that it could either be leaned up against the wall or else suspended from the ceiling on a silver chain. One of the boards of the top is gone, but I am told that that is of no consequence, as all the best specimens of Brittany tables have at least one board out.'

"Doesn't that sound fascinating, Charles? Do send Jane a cable at once not to miss it."

And when I took my leave a little later, I realized once and for all that the antique business is not for me.

(1926)

A Lesson on the Links

The Application of Mathematics to Golf

IT IS ONLY quite recently that I have taken up golf. In fact, I have only played for three or four years, and seldom more than ten games in a week or at most four in a day. I have only had a proper golf vest for two years: I only bought a "spoon" this year and I am not going to get Scotch socks till next year.

In short, I am still a beginner. I have once, it is true, had the distinction of "making a hole in one," in other words of hitting the ball into the pot, or can, or receptacle, in one shot. That is to say, after I had hit, a ball was found in the can and my ball was not found. It is what we call circumstantial evidence – the same thing that people are hanged for.

Under such circumstances I should have little to teach to anybody about golf. But it has occurred to me that from a certain angle my opinions may be of value. I at least bring to bear on the game all the resources of a trained mind and all the equipment of a complete education.

In particular I may be able to help the ordinary golfer – or "goofer" – others prefer "gopher" – by showing him something of the application of mathematics to golf.

Many a player is perhaps needlessly discouraged by not being able to calculate properly the chances and probabilities of progress in the game. Take, for example, the simple problem of "going round in bogey." The ordinary average player such as I am now becoming – something between a beginner and an expert – necessarily wonders to himself, "Shall I ever be able to go around in bogey; will the time ever come when I shall make not one hole in bogey, but all the holes?"

To this, according to my calculations, the answer is overwhelmingly "yes." The thing is a mere matter of time and patience.

Let me explain for the few people who never play golf (such as night watchmen, night clerks in hotels, night operators, astronomers and negroes), that "bogey" is an imaginary player who does each hole at golf in the fewest strokes that a first-class player with ordinary luck ought to need for that hole.

Now an ordinary player finds it quite usual to do one hole out of the nine "in bogey," – as we golfers, or rather, "us goofers," call it, – but he wonders whether it will ever be his fate to do all the nine holes of the course in bogey. To which we answer again with absolute assurance, he will.

The thing is a simple instance of what is called the mathematical theory of probability. If a player usually and generally makes one hole in bogey, or comes close to it, his chance of making any one particular hole in bogey is one in nine. Let us say, for easier calculation, that it is one in ten. When he makes it, his chance of doing the same with the next hole is also one in ten; therefore, taken from the start his chance of making the two holes successively in bogey is one-tenth of a tenth chance. In other words it is one in a hundred.

The reader sees already how encouraging the calculation is. Here is at last something definite about his progress. Let us carry it further. His chance of making three holes in bogey one after the other will be one in a thousand, his chance of four one in ten thousand and his chance of making the whole round in bogey will be exactly one in 1,000,000,000, – that is one in a billion games.

In other words, all he has to do is to keep right on. But for how long? he asks. How long will it take, playing the ordinary number of games in a month, to play a billion? Will it take several years? Yes, it will.

An ordinary player plays about 100 games in a year, and will therefore play a billion games in exactly 10,000,000 years. That gives us precisely the time it will need for persons like the reader and myself to go round in bogey.

Even this calculation needs a little revision. We have to allow for the fact that in 10,000,000 years the shrinking of the earth's crust, the diminishing heat of the sun and the general slackening down of the whole solar system, together with the passing of eclipses, comets and showers of meteors, may put us off our game.

In fact, I doubt if we shall ever get around in bogey.

Let us try something else. Here is a very interesting calculation in regard to "allowing for the wind."

I have noticed that a great many golf players of my own particular class are always preoccupied with the question of "allowing for the wind." My friend, Amphibius Jones, for example, just before driving always murmurs something, as if in prayer, about "allowing for the wind." After driving he says with a sigh, "I didn't allow for the wind." In fact, all through my class there is a general feeling that our game is practically ruined by the wind. We ought really to play in the middle of the desert of Sahara where there isn't any.

It occurred to me that it might be interesting to reduce to a formula the effect exercised by the resistance of the wind on a moving golf ball. For example, in our game of last Wednesday, Jones in his drive struck the ball with what he assures me was his full force, hitting in with absolute accuracy, as he himself admits, fair in the center, and he himself feeling, on his own assertion, absolutely fit, his eye being (a very necessary thing with Jones), absolutely "in," and he also having on his proper sweater, – a further necessary condition of first-class play. Under all the favorable circumstances the ball only advanced fifty yards! It was evident at once that it was a simple matter of the wind: the wind, which was of that treacherous character which blows over the links unnoticed, had impinged full upon the ball, pressed it backward and forced it to the earth.

Here then is a neat subject of calculation. Granted that Jones, – as measured on a hitting machine the week the circus was here, – can hit two tons and that this whole force was pressed against a golf ball only one inch and a quarter in diameter. What happens? My reader will remember that the superficial area of such a golf ball is 3.1415 times $\frac{5}{8}$ square inches multiplied by 4, or, more simply $4\pi r^2$. And all of this driven forward with the power of 4,000 pounds to the inch!

In short, taking Jones's statements at their face value the ball would have traveled, had it not been for the wind, no less than 6½ miles.

I give next a calculation of even more acute current interest. It is in regard to "moving the head." How often is an admirable stroke at golf spoiled by moving the head! I have seen members of our golf club sit silent and glum all evening, murmuring from time to time, "I moved my head." When Jones and I play together I often hit the ball sideways into the vegetable garden from which no ball returns (they have one of these on every links; it is a Scottish invention). And whenever I do so Jones always says, "You moved your head." In return when *he* drives his ball away up into air and down again ten yards in front of him, I always retaliate by saying, "You moved your head, old man."

In short, if absolute immobility of the head could be achieved the major problem of golf would be solved.

Let us put the theory mathematically. The head, poised on

he neck, has a circumferential sweep or orbit of about two inches, not counting the rolling of the eyes. The circumferential sweep of a golf ball is based on a radius of 250 yards, or a circumference of about 1,600 yards, which is very nearly equal to a mile. Inside this circumference is an area of 27,878,400 square feet, the whole of which is controlled by a tiny movement of the human neck. In other words, if a player were to wiggle his neck even 1/190 of an inch the amount of ground on which the ball might falsely alight would be half a million square feet. If at the same time he multiplies the effect by rolling his eyes, the ball might alight anywhere.

I feel certain that after reading this any sensible player will keep his head still.

A further calculation remains, – and one perhaps of even greater practical interest than the ones above.

Everybody who plays golf is well aware that on some days he plays better than on others. Question, – how often does a man really play his game?

I take the case of Amphibius Jones. There are certain days, when he is, as he admits himself, "*put off his game*" by not having on his proper golf vest. On other days the light puts him off his game; at other times the dark; so, too, the heat; or again the cold. He is often put off his game because he has been up too late the night before; or similarly because he has been to bed too early the night before; the barking of a dog always puts him off his game; so do children; or adults, or women. Bad news disturbs his game; so does good: so also does the absence of news.

All of this may be expressed mathematically by a very simple application of the theory of permutations and probability; let us say that there are altogether fifty forms of disturbance any one of which puts Jones off his game. Each one of these disturbances happens, say, once in ten days. What chance is there that a day will come when *not a single one of them occurs?* The formula is a little complicated but mathematicians will recognize the answer at once as $x/1 + x^2/1 \ldots x^n/1$. In fact, that is exactly how often Jones plays at his best $x/1 + x^2/1 \ldots x^n/1$ worked out in time and reckoning four game to the week and allowing for leap years and solar eclipses, i comes to about once in 2,930,000 years.

And from watching Jones play I think that this is abou right.

(1928)

Fifty Cents' Worth

"IS THAT MY Uncle William?" asks the inquirer. His voice trembles a little as he says it. It is costing him fifty cents to ask this. If it should turn out not to be Uncle William – which might surely happen among the myriads of the spirit world – the fifty cents would be a dead loss.

But luckily it turns out to be all right.

"Yes," says the voice of the medium. She is lying prostrate on a sofa in an attitude that resembles death, but she looks out of the corner of one eye. "Yes," she says, "it's Uncle William."

She is dressed in a figured robe, presumed to represent the symbols of Persian magic, and, on the business card that stands on the window-sill, her name appears as Abracadabra, the Persian Sorceress (fifty cents a séance). But when she speaks, or when the voice speaks through her, the accent of the communicating spirit is just plain, everyday English.

"Yes," she repeats, "it is Uncle William."

"And how are you, Uncle William? Are you happy?"

"Yes, very happy. It's all so bright and beautiful over here."

"That's good. Is Henry there?"

"Yes, Henry is beside me. Henry is happy too."

"I'm glad of that. Ask Henry if he remembers me."

"Yes, he says he does. He wants you to believe that he is very happy."

"Does he send any message?"

"Yes. He says to tell you that goodness is the only gladness, and you are to keep right on expanding yourself all you can."

"Good. Ask him if Martha is there?"

"Yes. He says that Martha is right there."

"Good. And ask him who else is with him there."

For the first time the medium pauses. She speaks with a certain hesitation, as if groping her way. The reason is, no doubt, that there is some kind of thought-block or stoppage in the ethereal wave. Either that or something in the form of the question. Or perhaps the chief cause of these hesitations, or stoppages, is that the ethereal thought-wave has momentarily slipped from one plane to another and not yet regeared itself to the vibration. Very likely, too, the zodiacal body or somatic double has for the moment passed through an obfuscation. It is certainly some simple thing of that sort.

Hence it comes about that, when the inquirer asks who else is over there with Uncle William, the medium pauses and gropes.

"It is not very clear," she says slowly. "There's a dimness. I see two figures, but perhaps there may be three. They look strangely alike, and yet oddly dissimilar. They seem to be dressed all in deep black, or else white – I can't quite be sure."

The sitter interrupts.

"Ask if they are Mary Ann and Pete," he says eagerly.

"Yes," says the medium, "they are! They are! Mary Ann is waving to you. Pete is waving. I can see them very plainly now."

"What are they saying?" asks the inquirer anxiously.

"They are saying that there is no light but eternity, and they want you to keep on getting on a higher and higher plane."

At this moment the proprietor of the Spiritualistic Parlours (Hours 9 to 12, 12 to 6, and 6 to 11.30) comes back into the room. His official name, on his cards, is Nadir the Nameless, the Persian Astrologer, and this is why his face is stained with tan shoe polish (rub well with the fingers, followed by a dry rag, etc.) But he, too, speaks plain English. He lays his finger on the shoulder of the inquirer and tells him that his time is up. His fifty cents' worth is exhausted.

So the inquirer, his interview terminated, goes back to his fellows. He will tell of what he has heard. He will tell it eight or ten times that evening and repeat it at intervals for days and months afterwards. He will say that it was the most marvellous thing he ever listened to. He will say the woman knew all the names of all his deceased relations, named them without hesitation, and told him all about them.

All this is what he will say.

And the more often he tells all this, the more completely the inquirer feels that the mystery of mysteries is solved.

But, in the meantime, when the interviewer has left the Parlour of the Spirits, Nadir the Nameless helps his wife to rise from the tawdry little couch.

Her face is weary and sad.

"You're tired, dear," says the Astrologer gently. "Come into the other room. I've made some tea."

"Ain't I seen that fellow here before?" asks the medium wearily.

"Yes, I think he was here one day last week," says Nadir. "But I'm not sure."

Nadir the Nameless and his wife don't keep elaborate track of their clients. There is a myth abroad that they follow them about and dig up all kinds of information about them in secret. They don't. Why should they? Uncle William is good enough.

"Look," says Nadir the Nameless, as they sit down in the back room, "I've got the supper all ready for you."

"You're so good, Fred," says the medium.

Then she begins to cry softly. "I was thinking of Nan," she says; "all day, while I was working, I was thinking of Nan."

Nan was the little daughter of Nadir the Nameless and Abracadabra, his wife. She died last week. But do they call her up from the spirit world? Ah, no! Leave that for Uncle William and such.

"Don't cry," says Nadir. "Wait while I go and take the card out of the window. You mustn't work any more to-day."

"But there's the rent, Fred," says the wife, pausing in her tears.

"Never mind; we'll manage somehow. And listen, dear, you take this fifty cents that that guy paid for his revelation and buy some flowers for Nan's grave. To-morrow's Sunday. Wait till I go and wash, and we'll have tea. Don't cry, dear. Don't cry."

And with this first and last of human consolations on his lips, he leaves her to herself.

(1929)

The Perfect Optimist

or Day-dreams in a Dental Chair

WELL, HERE we are again seated in the big red plush chair in for one of our jolly little mornings with our dentist. My! It certainly is cosy to settle back into this comfortable chair with a whole quiet morning in front of us – no work to do, no business to think of, just to lie in one of our comfortable day-dreams.

How pleasant it is in this chair, anyway, with the sunshine streaming in through the window upon us and illuminating every corner of the neat and immaculate little room in which we sit.

For immaculate neatness and cleanliness, I repeat, give me a little up-to-date dental room every time. Talk of your cosy libraries or your dens, they won't compare with this little nook. Here we are with everything we need around us, all within easy arm's-length reach. Here on this revolving tray are our pleasant little nippers, pincers and forceps, some so small and cute and others so big and strong that we feel a real confidence in them. They'd never let go of anything! Here is our dainty little electric buzzer with our revolving gimlets at the end; our little hammer on the left; our bradawl on the right – everything!

For the moment our dental friend is out of the room –

telephoning, we imagine. The merry fellow is so popular with all his friends that they seem to ring him up every few minutes.

Little scraps of his conversation reach our ears as we lie half-buried in our white towel, in a sweet reverie of expectancy.

"Pretty bad in the night, was it, eh? Well, perhaps you'd better come along down and we'll make a boring through that bicuspid and see what's there!"

Full of ideas, he is, always like that – never discouraged, something new to suggest all the time. And then we hear him say: "Well, let me see. I'm busy now for about a couple of hours —" Hurrah! That means us! We were so afraid he was going to say, "I'll be through here in about five minutes." But no, it's all right; we've got two long, dreamy hours in front of us.

He comes back into the room and his cheery presence, as he searches among his instruments and gives a preliminary buzz to the buzzer, seems to make the sunshine even brighter. How pleasant life seems – the dear old life; that is, the life we quitted ten minutes ago and to which, please Providence, we hope to return in two hours. We never felt till we sat here how full and pleasant life is. Think of it, the simple joy of being alive. That's all we ask – of going to work each day (without a toothache) and coming home each night to eat our dinner. If only people realized it – just to live in our world without a toothache. . . .

So runs our pleasant reverie. But, meanwhile, our dental friend has taken up a little hammer and has tapped us, in his playful way, on the back teeth.

"Feel that?" he asks.

And he's right, the merry dog! We *do* feel it. He guessed it right away. We are hoping so much that he will hit us again.

Come on, let's have a little more fun like that. But no. He's laid aside his hammer and as nearly as we can see has rolled up his cuffs to the elbow and has started his good old electric buzzer into a roar.

Ah, ha! Now we are going to get something – this is going to be the big fun, the real thing. That's the greatest thing about our little dental mornings, there's always something new. Always as we sit we have a pleasant expectancy that our dental friend is planning a new one.

Now, then, let us sit back tight, while he drives at our jaw with the buzzer. Of all the exhilarating feelings of hand-to-hand conflict, of man against man, of mind matched against mind, and intelligence pitted against intelligence, I know of none more stimulating than when we brace ourselves for this conflict of man and machinery. He has on his side the power of electricity and the force of machinery.

But we are not without resource. We brace ourselves, laughingly, in our chair while he starts to bore. We need, in fact, our full strength; but, on the other hand, if he tries to keep up at this pace his hands will get tired. We realize, with a sense of amusement, that if his machine slips, he may get a nasty thump on the hand against our jawbone.

He slacks off for just a second – half withdraws his machine and says, "Were you at the football match yesterday?" and then starts his instrument again at full roar.

"Were we at the football match yesterday?" How strange it sounds! "Why, yes, of course we were!" In that far-away long-ago world where they play football and where there is no toothache – we were there only yesterday afternoon.

Yes, we remember, it was just towards the end of that game that we felt those twinges in one of the – what does he call it, the lower molars? Anyway, one of those twinges which started the exultant idea racing through our minds, "Tomorrow we'll have to go to the dentist."

A female voice speaking into the room has called him to the telephone, and again we are alone. What if he never comes back!

The awful thought leaps to our minds, what if he comes in and says, "I'm sorry to say I have to take a train out of town at once." How terrible!

Perhaps he'll come in and say, "Excuse me, I have to leave instantly for Canada!" or, "I'll have to let your work go; they've sent for me to go to China!"

But no, how lucky! Back he comes again. We've not lost him. And now what is he at? Stuffing cotton-wool up into our head, wool saturated with some kind of drugs, and pounding it in with a little hammer.

And then – all of a sudden, so it seems – he steps back and says, "There, that will do nicely till Monday!" And we rise half-dazed from our chair to realize in our disappointment that it is over already. Somehow we had thought that our pleasant drowsy morning of pounding and boring and dreaming in the sunlight, while our dental friend mixed up something new, would last for ever. And now, all of a sudden, it is over.

Never mind! After all, he said Monday! It won't seem so long till then! And meantime we can think about it all day and look forward to it and imagine how it is going to feel. Oh! It won't be long.

And so we step out into the street – full of cotton-wool and drugs and electricity and reverie – like a person returning to a forgotten world and dazed to find it there.

(1932)

Ho for Happiness

A Plea for Lighter and Brighter Literature

"WHY IS IT," said some one in conversation the other day, "that all the really good short stories seem to contain so much sadness and suffering and to turn so much on crime and wickedness? Why can't they be happy all the time?"

No one present was able to answer the question. But I thought it over afterwards, and I think I see why it is so. A happy story, after all, would make pretty dull reading. It may be all right in real life to have everything come along just right, with happiness and good luck all the time, but in fiction it would never do.

Stop, let me illustrate the idea. Let us make up a story which is happy all the time and contrast it as it goes along with the way things happen in the really good stories.

Harold Herald never forgot the bright October morning when the mysterious letter, which was to alter his whole life, arrived at his downtown office.

His stenographer brought it in to him and laid it on his desk.

"A letter for you," she said. Then she kissed him and went out again.

Harold sat for some time with the letter in front of him. Should he open it? After all, why not?

He opened the letter. Then the idea occurred to him to read it. "I might as well," he thought.

"Dear Mr. Herald" (so ran the letter), "if you will have the kindness to call at this office, we shall be happy to tell you something to your great advantage."

The letter was signed John Scribman. The paper on which it was written bore the heading "Scribman, Scribman & Company, Barristers, Solicitors, etc., No. 13 Yonge St."

A few moments later saw Harold on his way to the lawyers' office. Never had the streets looked brighter and more cheerful than in this perfect October sunshine. In fact, they never had been.

Nor did Harold's heart misgive him and a sudden suspicion enter his mind as Mr. Scribman, the senior partner, rose from his chair to greet him. Not at all. Mr. Scribman was a pleasant, middle-aged man whose countenance behind his gold spectacles beamed with goodwill and good nature.

"Ah, Mr. Harold Herald," he said, "or perhaps, you will let me call you simply Harold. I didn't like to give you too much news in one short letter. The fact is that our firm has been entrusted to deliver to you a legacy, or rather a gift. . . . Stop, stop!" continued the lawyer, as Harold was about to interrupt with questions, ". . . our client's one request was that his name would not be divulged. He thought it would be so much nicer for you just to have the money and not know who gave it to you."

Harold murmured his assent.

Mr. Scribman pushed a bell.

"Mr. Harold Herald's money, if you please," he said.

A beautiful stenographer wearing an American Beauty rose at her waist entered the room carrying a silken bag.

"There is half a million dollars here in five-hundred-dollar bills," said the lawyer. "At least, we didn't count them, but that is what our client said. Did you take any?" he asked the stenographer.

"I took out a few last night to go to the theatre with," admitted the girl with a pretty blush.

"Monkey!" said Mr. Scribman. "But that's all right. Don't bother with a receipt, Harold. Come along with me: my daughter is waiting for us down below in the car to take us to lunch."

Harold thought he had never seen a more beautiful girl than Alicia Scribman. In fact he hadn't. The luxurious motor, the faultless chauffeur, the presence of the girl beside him and the bag of currency under the seat, the sunlit streets filled with happy people with the bright feeling of just going back to work, full of lunch – the sight of all this made Harold feel as if life were indeed a pleasant thing.

"After all," he mused, "how little is needed for our happiness! Half a million dollars, a motor-car, a beautiful girl, youth, health – surely one can be content with that . . ."

It was after lunch at the beautiful country home of the Scribmans that Harold found himself alone for a few minutes with Miss Scribman.

He rose, walked over to her and took her hand, kneeling on one knee and pulling up his pants so as not to make a crease in them.

"Alicia!" he said. "Ever since I first saw you, I have loved you. I want to ask you if you will marry me?"

"Oh, Harold," said Alicia, leaning forward and putting both her arms about his neck with one ear against the upper right-hand end of his cheekbone. "Oh, Harold!"

"I can, as you know," continued Harold, "easily support you."

"Oh, that's all right," said Alicia. "As a matter of fact, I have much more than that of my own, to be paid over to me when I marry."

"Then you will marry me?" said Harold rapturously.

"Yes, indeed," said Alicia, "and it happens so fortunately just now, as papa himself is engaged to marry again and so I shall be glad to have a new home of my own. Papa is marrying a charming girl, but she is so much younger than he is that perhaps she would not want a grown-up stepdaughter."

Harold made his way back to the city in a tumult of happiness. Only for a moment was his delirium of joy brought to a temporary standstill.

As he returned to his own apartment, he suddenly remembered that he was engaged to be married to his cousin Winnie. . . . The thing had been entirely washed out of his mind by the flood-tide of his joy.

He seized the telephone.

"Winnie," he said, "I am so terribly sorry. I want to ask you to release me from our engagement. I want to marry someone else."

"That's all right, Hal!" came back Winnie's voice cheerfully. "As a matter of fact, I want to do the same thing myself. I got engaged last week to the most charming man in the world, a little older, in fact quite a bit older than I am, but ever so nice. He is a wealthy lawyer and his name is Walter Scribman. . . ."

The double wedding took place two weeks later, the church being smothered with chrysanthemums and the clergyman buried under Canadian currency. Harold and Alicia built a beautiful country home at the other side – the farthest-away side – of the city from the Scribmans'. A year or so after their marriage, they had a beautiful boy, and then another, then a couple of girls (twins), and then they lost count.

There. Pretty dull reading it makes. And yet, I don't know. There's something about it, too. In the real stories Mr. Scribman would have been a crook, and Harold would have either murdered Winnie or been accused of it, and the stenographer with the rose would have stolen the money instead of just taking it, and it wouldn't have happened in bright, clear October weather but in dirty old November – oh, no, let us have romance and happiness, after all. It may not be true, but it's better.

(1932)

My Remarkable Uncle

A Personal Document

THE MOST remarkable man I have ever known in my life was my uncle Edward Philip Leacock – known to ever so many people in Winnipeg fifty or sixty years ago as E.P. His character was so exceptional that it needs nothing but plain narration. It was so exaggerated already that you couldn't exaggerate it.

When I was a boy of six, my father brought us, a family flock, to settle on an Ontario farm. We lived in an isolation unknown, in these days of radio, anywhere in the world. We were thirty-five miles from a railway. There were no newspapers. Nobody came and went. There was nowhere to come and go. In the solitude of the dark winter nights the stillness was that of eternity.

Into this isolation there broke, two years later, my dynamic Uncle Edward, my father's younger brother. He had just come from a year's travel around the Mediterranean. He must have been about twenty-eight, but seemed a more than adult man, bronzed and self-confident, with a square beard like a Plantagenet King. His talk was of Algiers, of the African slave market; of the Golden Horn and the Pyramids. To us it sounded like the *Arabian Nights.* When we asked, "Uncle Edward, do

you know the Prince of Wales?" he answered, "Quite inti-
mately" – with no further explanation. It was an impressive
trick he had.

In that year, 1878, there was a general election in Canada. E.P.
was in it up to the neck in less than no time. He picked up
the history and politics of Upper Canada in a day, and in a
week knew everybody in the countryside. He spoke at every
meeting, but his strong point was the personal contact of
electioneering, of bar-room treats. This gave full scope for his
marvellous talent for flattery and make-believe.

"Why, let me see" – he would say to some tattered country
specimen beside him glass in hand – "surely, if your name is
Framley, you must be a relation of my dear old friend General
Sir Charles Framley of the Horse Artillery?" "Mebbe," the flat-
tered specimen would answer. "I guess, mebbe; I ain't kept
track very good of my folks in the old country." "Dear me! I
must tell Sir Charles that I've seen you. He'll be so pleased."
. . . In this way in a fortnight E.P. had conferred honours and
distinctions on half the township of Georgina. They lived in a
recaptured atmosphere of generals, admirals and earls. Vote?
How else could they vote than conservative, men of family like
them?

It goes without saying that in politics, then and always, E.P.
was on the conservative, the *aristocratic* side, but along with
that was hail-fellow-well-met with the humblest. This was
instinct. A democrat can't condescend. He's down already.
But when a conservative stoops, he conquers.

The election, of course, was a walk-over. E.P. might have
stayed to reap the fruits. But he knew better. Ontario at that
day was too small a horizon. For these were the days of the
hard times of Ontario farming, when mortgages fell like

snowflakes, and farmers were sold up, or sold out, or went "to the States," or faded humbly underground.

But all the talk was of Manitoba now opening up. Nothing would do E.P. but that he and my father must go west. So we had a sale of our farm, with refreshments, old-time fashion, for the buyers. The poor, lean cattle and the broken machines fetched less than the price of the whisky. But E.P. laughed it all off, quoted that the star of the Empire glittered in the west, and off to the West they went, leaving us children behind at school.

They hit Winnipeg just on the rise of the boom, and E.P. came at once into his own and rode on the crest of the wave. There is something of magic appeal in the rush and movement of a "boom" town – a Winnipeg of the 80's, a Carson City of the 60's. . . . Life comes to a focus; it is all here and now, all *present*, no past and no outside – just a clatter of hammers and saws, rounds of drinks and rolls of money. In such an atmosphere every man seems a remarkable fellow, a man of exception; individuality separates out and character blossoms like a rose.

E.P. came into his own. In less than no time he was in everything and knew everybody, conferring titles and honours up and down Portage Avenue. In six months he had a great fortune, on paper; took a trip east and brought back a charming wife from Toronto; built a large house beside the river; filled it with pictures that he said were his ancestors, and carried on in it a roaring hospitality that never stopped.

His activities were wide. He was president of a bank (that never opened), head of a brewery (for brewing the Red River) and, above all, secretary-treasurer of the Winnipeg Hudson Bay and Arctic Ocean Railway that had a charter authorizing it to build a road to the Arctic Ocean, when it got ready. They had no track, but they printed stationery and passes, and in return E.P. received passes over all North America.

But naturally his main hold was politics. He was elected right away into the Manitoba Legislature. They would have made him Prime Minister but for the existence of the grand old man of the province, John Norquay. But even at that in a very short time Norquay ate out of E.P.'s hand, and E.P. led him on a string. I remember how they came down to Toronto, when I was a schoolboy, with an adherent group of "Westerners," all in heavy buffalo coats and bearded like Assyrians. E.P. paraded them on King Street like a returned explorer with savages.

Naturally E.P.'s politics remained conservative. But he pitched the note higher. Even the ancestors weren't good enough. He invented a Portuguese Dukedom (some one of our family once worked in Portugal) – and he conferred it, by some kind of reversion, on my elder brother Jim who had gone to Winnipeg to work in E.P.'s office. This enabled him to say to visitors in his big house, after looking at the ancestors – to say in a half-whisper behind his hand, "Strange to think that two deaths would make that boy a Portuguese Duke." But Jim never knew which two Portuguese to kill.

To aristocracy E.P. also added a touch of peculiar prestige by always being apparently just about to be called away – imperially. If someone said, "Will you be in Winnipeg all winter, Mr. Leacock?" he answered, "It will depend a good deal on what happens in West Africa." Just that; West Africa beat them.

Then came the crash of the Manitoba boom. Simple people, like my father, were wiped out in a day. Not so E.P. The crash just gave him a lift as the smash of a big wave lifts a strong swimmer. He just went right on. I believe that in reality he was left utterly bankrupt. But it made no difference. He used credit instead of cash. He still had his imaginary bank, and his railway to the Arctic Ocean. Hospitality still roared and the tradesmen still paid for it. Any one who called about a bill was told that E.P.'s movements were uncertain and would depend a good deal on what happened in Johannesburg. That held them another six months.

It was during this period that I used to see him when he made his periodic trips "east," to impress his creditors in the West. He floated, at first very easily, on hotel credit, borrowed loans and unpaid bills. A banker, especially a country town banker, was his natural mark and victim. He would tremble as E.P. came in, like a stock-dove that sees a hawk. E.P.'s method was so simple; it was like showing a farmer peas under thimbles. As he entered the banker's side-office he would say: "I say. Do you fish? Surely that's a greenhart casting-rod on the wall?" (E. P. knew the names of everything.) In a few minutes the banker, flushed and pleased, was exhibiting the rod, and showing flies in a box out of a drawer. When E.P. went out he carried a hundred dollars with him. There was no security. The transaction was all over.

He dealt similarly with credit, with hotels, livery stables and bills in shops. They all fell for his method. He bought with lavish generosity, never asking a price. He never suggested pay till just as an afterthought, just as he was going out. And then: "By the way, please let me have the account promptly. I may be going away," and, in an aside to me, as if not meant for the shop, "Sir Henry Loch has cabled again from West Africa." And so out; they had never seen him before; nor since.

The proceeding with a hotel was different. A country hotel was, of course, easy, in fact too easy. E. P. would sometimes pay such a bill in cash, just as a sportsman won't shoot a sitting partridge. But a large hotel was another thing. E.P., on leaving – that is, when all ready to leave, coat, bag and all – would call for his bill at the desk. At the sight of it he would break out into enthusiasm at the reasonableness of it. "Just think!" he would say in his "aside" to me, "compare that with the Hotel Crillon in Paris!" The hotel proprietor had no way of doing this; he just felt that he ran a cheap hotel. Then another "aside," "Do remind me to mention to Sir John how admirably we've been treated; he's coming here next week." "Sir John" was our Prime Minister and the hotel keeper hadn't known he was coming – and he wasn't. . . . Then came the final touch – "Now, let me see . . . seventy-six dollars . . . seventy-six. . . . You give me" – and E.P. fixed his eye firmly on the hotel man – "give me twenty-four dollars, and then I can remember to send an even hundred." The man's hand trembled. But he gave it.

This does not mean that E.P. was in any sense a crook, in any degree dishonest. His bills to him were just "deferred pay," like the British debts to the United States. He never did, never contemplated, a crooked deal in his life. All his grand schemes were as open as sunlight – and as empty.

In all his interviews E.P. could fashion his talk to his audience. On one of his appearances I introduced him to a group of college friends, young men near to degrees, to whom degrees mean everything. In casual conversation E.P. turned to me and said, "Oh, by the way you'll be glad to know that I've just received my honorary degree from the Vatican – at last!" The "at last" was a knock-out – a degree from the Pope, and over-due at that!

Of course it could not last. Gradually credit crumbles. Faith weakens. Creditors grow hard, and friends turn their faces away. Gradually E.P. sank down. The death of his wife had left him a widower, a shuffling, half-shabby figure, familiar on the street, that would have been pathetic but for his indomitable self-belief, the illumination of his mind. Even at that, times grew hard with him. At length even the simple credit of the bar-rooms broke under him. I have been told by my brother Jim – the Portuguese Duke – of E.P. being put out of a Winni-peg bar, by an angry bar-tender who at last broke the mesmer-ism. E.P. had brought in a little group, spread up the fingers of one hand and said, "Mr. Leacock, five!" . . . The bar-tender broke into oaths. E.P. hooked a friend by the arm. "Come away," he said. "I'm afraid the poor fellow's crazy! But I hate to report him."

Presently even his power to travel came to an end. The rail-ways found out at last that there wasn't any Arctic Ocean, and anyway the printer wouldn't print.

Just once again he managed to "come east." It was in June 1891. I met him forging along King Street in Toronto – a trifle shabby but with a plug hat with a big band of crape round it. "Poor Sir John," he said. "I felt I simply must come down for his funeral." Then I remembered that the Prime Minister was dead, and realized that kindly sentiment had meant free transportation.

That was the last I ever saw of E.P. A little after that some one paid his fare back to England. He received, from some family trust, a little income of perhaps two pounds a week. On that he lived, with such dignity as might be, in a lost village in Worcestershire. He told the people of the village – so I learned later – that his stay was uncertain; it would depend a good deal on what happened in China. But nothing happened in China; there he stayed, years and years. There he might have finished out, but for a strange chance of fortune, a sort of poetic justice, that gave E.P. an evening in the sunset.

It happened that in the part of England where our family belonged there was an ancient religious brotherhood, with a monastery and dilapidated estates that went back for centuries. E.P. descended on them, the brothers seeming to him an easy mark, as brothers indeed are. In the course of his pious "retreat," E.P. took a look into the brothers' finances, and his quick intelligence discovered an old claim against the British Government, large in amount and valid beyond a doubt.

In less than no time E.P. was at Westminster, representing the brothers. He knew exactly how to handle British officials; they were easier even than Ontario hotel keepers. All that is needed is hints of marvellous investment overseas. They never go there but they remember how they just missed Johannesburg or were just late on Persian oil. All E.P. needed was his Arctic Railway. "When you come out, I must take you over our railway. I really think that as soon as we reached the Coppermine River we must put the shares on here; it's too big for New York. . . ."

So E.P. got what he wanted. The British Government are so used to old claims that it would as soon pay as not. There are plenty left.

The brothers got a whole lot of money. In gratitude they invited E.P. to be their permanent manager; so there he was, lifted into ease and affluence. The years went easily by, among gardens, orchards and fishponds old as the Crusades.

When I was lecturing in London in 1921 he wrote to me: "Do come down; I am too old now to travel; but any day you like I will send a chauffeur with a car and two lay-brothers to bring you down." I thought the "lay-brothers" a fine touch – just like E.P.

I couldn't go. I never saw him again. He ended out his days at the monastery, no cable calling him to West Africa. Years ago I used to think of E.P. as a sort of humbug, a source of humour. Looking back now I realize better the unbeatable quality of his spirit, the mark, we like to think just now, of the British race.

If there is a paradise, I am sure he will get in. He will say at the gate – "Peter? Then surely you must be a relation of Lord Peter of Tichfield?"

But if he fails, then, as the Spaniards say so fittingly, "May the earth lie light upon him."

(1941)

Good News! A New Party!

("The old-time political parties, gentlemen, have had their day. What we need is new life, new energy and, above all, if I may say so, a new Working of the Spirit." – From any soapbox, Halifax to California.)

IT IS A great pleasure – indeed it gives me a thrill – to be able to announce to the public through the kindly medium of this volume that at last the New Party has come! The hope, the promise, contained in such words as those above is fulfilled. The thing is here. I saw its inception. I was present at it myself no later than last night. All that is now needed is to keep it incepted . . .

Now, please, don't ask me for details, for names and places and all that; everything will appear in the full publicity of the newspapers.

It came about this way. I'm not in politics but I have many friends who are – some on one side, some on the other, some on both . . . naturally I hear of the new movements. So when Hoggitt called on the phone to me to come down and join him at the Piccadilly I knew that the big stuff was on.

I found him there at a table and he began to talk, right away and with the greatest enthusiasm, about the new Party. You know Hoggitt. He's all right. He's got a sort of fierce way of talking, but he's all right. He's a big dark fellow and he always seems to be threatening but he isn't – that is, he *is* in a way, but he's all right. Anyway I'd no sooner sat down than he was talking full speed of the Party – with a sort of inspiration.

"It's the real thing," he said, "it's based on human sympathy and equality – where's that damn waiter? We're aiming at what the old parties never had – social cohesion – I'd like to fire that fellow – and the right of every man to a voice . . . gimme that check and don't talk back to me . . ."

He was still muttering at the waiter when we left . . .

"We'll drive along to the meeting," he said.

But, of course, we couldn't get a taxi; we waited – say, we must have waited four minutes; anyway Hoggitt said, "Oh come along. There's no use waiting for a taxi; these taxi fellers just go beyond all limits . . . and *money*! What they're making now! I don't know what they get, but, by gosh, a mighty comfortable living, I'll say! It's a scandal."

So we walked. In any case it was only four blocks and I was glad because it gave Hoggitt a chance to explain to me all about the new party. I must say it sounded fine – no more of that miserable intrigue and crookedness of the old parties . . . things done in the dark . . . no more leaning on the "interests" for money; just straight honesty. Hoggitt said that when we got to the hall he'd introduce me to the chairman, but not to pay too much attention to him as they were going to ease him out. Of course he doesn't know it. They'll keep him while they still need him. Hoggitt said he's not sufficiently genial – that was it – or, no, I've got it wrong – *too* genial.

The meeting was in a pretty big hall. There must have been well over a hundred, most of them smoking and standing round. They looked all right, too. I've been to a good many political meetings but I couldn't see anything wrong with them. Some of them looked mighty decent fellers, you know – educated – not like what you'd imagine at all. It seemed a kind of free and easy crowd. The chairman was just going to the platform so I only had time to shake hands with him, a middle aged looking man, quite well dressed – in fact I couldn't see a thing wrong with him.

Anyway he got up to talk, but they didn't listen much; they went on talking in groups round the room. Hoggitt said that's the way they do; they find they can get through more business if they don't listen. Hoggitt says that's the curse of Washington and Ottawa – one of them; he named quite a few.

The chairman was talking about the name of the party. He said, "Gentlemen, you'll be glad to know we've succeeded in getting a name for our party. You remember last week our difficulty over the proposal to christen the party the Forward Party . . ."

There was noise and applause which Hoggitt explained to me was because some of the members – people of fine old families who'd never moved since they came to America – thought that the Backward Party would be better, a finer ideal.

"We tried," the chairman went on, "both the name Forward Party and the name Backward Party, and, as you recall, the name Backwards-and-Forwards Party. We wanted something that would mean progressive and yet mean conservative . . . but we couldn't get it . . . We left, as you will remember, a committee sitting on it and they sat, at the Piccadilly, all that night but failed to find it. I'm glad to say that there has since come in the brilliant suggestion of a member – I won't name him – but you all know him, who gives us the title *The Non-Party Party* . . ."

Great applause . . . and cries . . . "Carried! Carried!"

Hoggitt explained to me on the side that the name came from Prof. Woodstick, Professor of Greek, who's in the party. In fact some of them call him the "brains of the party." Hoggitt thinks they'll probably have to drop him. People don't like the idea of brains running a party. Look at Washington or at

Ottawa – at the successful parties. Still I'll say in favor of Professor Woodstick, he doesn't *look* educated . . .

The chairman came and sat with us, while a man – I didn't catch his name – was talking on what shall we do to get the farmer's vote. It seems he's a member of the platform committee (subsection farming), but Mr. Mills the chairman says they'll probably have to shift him off. He looks too countrified. Anyway nobody listened much. He was talking mostly about his own little place out near Knowlton – no, I've got that wrong, – out past Knowlton; he said he wouldn't call it exactly a farm, but we could call it a farm if we liked, so I called it a farm. It appears he grows a lot of stuff on it, more lettuce, for instance, than his wife can eat, in fact, nearly enough for the horse . . . Well, you know what farm talk is at political meetings; he asked how many had seen the new type of dry silo? They hadn't . . .

But what he got to at length was the committee platform to catch the farm interest. I saw right away it was certainly good – "to give to all farmers a proper aggregate share of their own produce." That's the very thing to attract farmers. Someone wanted to insert the word "just" to make it read a "just share." But it was explained that the Liberals gave them that. They've had that since 1896.

There was a lot of unanimity and good feeling over that but on the other hand a lot of difficulty over the question of labor. The man who got up to talk (I didn't catch his name, something like Fitkin, or Delbosse – a name like that) – anyway, he said he was a lawyer and couldn't pretend to speak of labor but he said he had the deepest sympathy for labor but all the same it was hard even for a lawyer to get a formula to satisfy labor. A lot of the labor men now, he explained, are mighty well educated and it's hard to put anything past them; difficult to find words for a platform that they wouldn't see through. He'd made, he said, a conscientious attempt at some honest direct statement but everything seemed to have the same fault of giving away its meaning. He had had with him on the committee, he said, the Reverend Canon Sip . . .

There was applause at that, because everybody knows the Canon, and he was sitting right there anyway. Hoggitt explained that they had tried to keep him away but they failed; Hoggitt says it's all right to talk of popularity but the Canon makes a bad impression – too damn simple and friendly, Hoggitt said. "It won't go over with the plain people . . ."

Well, he'd had with him, the lawyer said, Canon Sip and their friend Mr. Vault who as they all knew was a bank manager, or rather an ex-bank manager, whom we were all glad to see back again with us, but with all that the three of them could do, it was hard to find any adequate words that wouldn't right away show what was meant. It was no use, he said, to advocate a "just reward" for labor. That might be all right for farmers, probably too much, but labor would see through it right away. But he was glad to say that Canon Sip had suggested a labor platform that he believed would carry the country. "We propose to give to labor everywhere an entire freedom from work."

There was a lot of applause, and I must say I realized the party had hit it this time – here you had all the old slogans, "freedom to work" and "freedom of work" subsumed – that was the word the speaker used – into one lucid thought.

It was a great hit for the Canon – no wonder he's popular. You see he's not a bit like what you'd expect from a religious man – he's always cheerful, takes a drink any time, in fact he was quite tight at Peggy Sherar's wedding the other day – smokes a cigar, indeed as someone said at the meeting, he just seems the ideal of an early Christian, you know, the kind they used to burn at Rome. All the same, some of them are a little afraid of it. They say if people get the idea that a party stands for religion, it's all over with it. So Mills and Hoggitt both talk of easing Canon Sip out of the party. They would, except that having him may help to bring in the liquor interest. It seems you can't possibly hope to get anything out of the liquor interest unless you have with you some sort of showing of clergymen and professors. Lawyers don't help much for that.

Mentioning that reminds me of the main thing of the evening, the really crucial stuff, when they all sat and listened – the discussion of ways and means, how to get money to carry on.

The chairman of the interim finance committee read a report which he prefaced with a repetition of last week's general resolution in favor of fair and open means of raising funds, without secrecy or subservience to moneyed interest. He said the committee had been at work. But he said, gentlemen, before you can get to fair and open means you've got to do a good lot of spade work underground in the dark. The committee, he said, had been hard at this. The time, he said, was not ripe to say what they had been doing. But they had not been idle. They had approached already three of our largest banks for financial support, with gratifying results. The first had invited them to come back in a month; the second, to come back in three months; the third had invited them never to come back. This, on the whole, was gratifying. They had got in touch with several manufacturing interests; one of the members of this committee knew personally very well the head of one of these interests – or rather, knew a lot about him – and had already obtained in this way his pledge to give as much as he has to.

They had done their best in the direction of both the liquor interests and the churches. But as members present would realize, it is very hard to attract the interest of these unless you get them together. They go, as we all know, hand in hand. Any large, really large, contribution from a liquor source will bring the clergy round us at once.

Meanwhile any members who would care before they passed out to leave a small party donation would find Mr. Sibley the treasurer at the table here. He added that Mr. Sibley had ink and a blank cheque book. But it was too bad. A lot of them were moving out already and I don't think they heard about Mr. Sibley having the cheque book.

I was driven home after the meeting by one of the younger members who had a car – a college boy, keen as anything on politics, enthusiastic and, I could see by his talk, straight as a string. He said he thought there were too many older men in the thing; he was trying to engineer an inside group of young men to get them out. That was queer, wasn't it? Because Hoggitt had told me they'd have to get rid of a lot of the younger men . . .

Anyway, there's no doubt what the party means.

(1943)

Humour As I See It

IT IS ONLY fair that at the back of this book I should be allowed a few pages to myself to put down some things that I really think.

Until two weeks ago I might have taken my pen in hand to write about humour with the confident air of an acknowledged professional.

But that time is past. Such claim as I had has been taken from me. In fact I stand unmasked. An English reviewer writing in a literary journal, the very name of which is enough to put contradiction to sleep, has said of my writing, "What is there, after all, in Professor Leacock's humour but a rather ingenious mixture of hyperbole and myosis?"

The man was right. How he stumbled upon this trade secret, I do not know. But I am willing to admit, since the truth is out, that it has long been my custom in preparing an article of a humorous nature to go down to the cellar and mix up half a gallon of myosis with a pint of hyperbole. If I want to give the article a decidedly literary character, I find it well to put in about half a pint of paresis. The whole thing is amazingly simple.

But I only mention this by way of introduction and to dispel any idea that I am conceited enough to write about humour, with the professional authority of Ella Wheeler Wilcox writing about love, or Eva Tanguay talking about dancing.

All that I dare claim is that I have as much sense of humour as other people. And, oddly enough, I notice that everybody else makes this same claim. Any man will admit, if need be, that his sight is not good, or that he cannot swim, or shoots badly with a rifle, but to touch upon his sense of humour is to give him a mortal affront.

"No," said a friend of mine the other day, "I never go to Grand Opera," and then he added with an air of pride – "You see, I have absolutely no ear for music."

"You don't say so!" I exclaimed.

"None!" he went on. "I can't tell one tune from another. I don't know *Home Sweet Home* from *God, Save the King*. I can't tell whether a man is tuning a violin or playing a sonata."

He seemed to get prouder and prouder over each item of his own deficiency. He ended by saying that he had a dog at his house that had a far better ear for music than he had. As soon as his wife or any visitor started to play the piano the dog always began to howl – plaintively, he said, as if it were hurt. He himself never did this.

When he had finished I made what I thought a harmless comment.

"I suppose," I said, "that you find your sense of humour deficient in the same way: the two generally go together."

My friend was livid with rage in a moment.

"Sense of humour!" he said. "My sense of humour! Me without a sense of humour! Why, I suppose I've a keener sense of humour than any man, or any two men, in this city!"

From that he turned to bitter personal attack. He said that *my* sense of humour seemed to have withered altogether.

He left me, still quivering with indignation.

Personally, however, I do not mind making the admission, however damaging it may be, that there are certain forms of so-called humour, or, at least, fun, which I am quite unable to appreciate. Chief among these is that ancient thing called the Practical Joke.

"You never knew McGann, did you?" a friend of mine asked me the other day. When I said "No, I had never known McGann," he shook his head with a sigh, and said:

"Ah, you should have known McGann. He had the greatest sense of humour of any man I ever knew – always full of jokes. I remember one night at the boarding house where we were, he stretched a string across the passageway and then rang the dinner bell. One of the boarders broke his leg. We nearly died laughing."

"Dear me!" I said. "What a humorist! Did he often do things like that?"

"Oh, yes, he was at them all the time. He used to put tar in the tomato soup, and beeswax and tin-tacks on the chairs. He was full of ideas. They seemed to come to him without any trouble."

McGann, I understand, is dead. I am not sorry for it. Indeed I think that for most of us the time has gone by when we can see the fun of putting tacks on chairs, or thistles in beds, or live snakes in people's boots.

To me it has always seemed that the very essence of good humour is that it must be without harm and without malice. I admit that there is in all of us a certain vein of the old original demoniacal humour or joy in the misfortune of another which sticks to us like our original sin. It ought not to be funny to see a man, especially a fat and pompous man, slip suddenly on a banana skin. But it is. When a skater on a pond who is describing graceful circles and showing off before the crowd, breaks through the ice and gets a ducking, everybody shouts with joy. To the original savage, the cream of the joke in such cases was found if the man who slipped broke his neck, or the man who went through the ice never came up again. I can imagine a group of pre-historic men standing round the ice-hole where he had disappeared and laughing till their sides split. If there had been such a thing as a pre-historic newspaper, the affair would have been headed up: "*Amusing Incident. Unknown Gentleman Breaks Through Ice and Is Drowned.*"

But our sense of humour under civilisation has been weakened. Much of the fun of this sort of thing has been lost on us.

Children, however, still retain a large share of this primitive sense of enjoyment.

I remember once watching two little boys making snowballs at the side of the street and getting ready a little store of them to use. As they worked there came along an old man wearing a silk hat, and belonging by appearance to the class of "jolly old gentlemen." When he saw the boys his gold spectacles gleamed with kindly enjoyment. He began waving his arms and calling, "Now, then, boys, free shot at me! free shot!" In his gaiety he had, without noticing it, edged himself over the sidewalk on to the street. An express cart collided with him and knocked him over on his back in a heap of snow. He lay there gasping and trying to get the snow off his face and spectacles. The boys gathered up their snow-balls and took a run towards him. "Free shot!" they yelled. "Soak him! Soak him!"

I repeat, however, that for me, as I suppose for most of us, it is a prime condition of humour that it must be without harm or malice, nor should it convey even incidentally any real picture of sorrow or suffering or death. There is a great deal in the humour of Scotland (I admit its general merit) which seems to me, not being a Scotchman, to sin in this respect. Take this familiar story (I quote it as something already known and not for the sake of telling it).

A Scotchman had a sister-in-law – his wife's sister – with whom he could never agree. He always objected to going anywhere with her, and in spite of his wife's entreaties always refused to do so. The wife was taken mortally ill and as she lay dying, she whispered, "John, ye'll drive Janet with you to the funeral, will ye no?" The Scotchman, after an internal struggle, answered, "Margaret, I'll do it for ye, but it'll spoil my day."

Whatever humour there may be in this is lost for me by the actual and vivid picture that it conjures up – the dying wife, the darkened room and the last whispered request.

No doubt the Scotch see things differently. That wonderful people – whom personally I cannot too much admire – always seem to me to prefer adversity to sunshine, to welcome the prospect of a pretty general damnation, and to live with grim cheerfulness within the very shadow of death. Alone among the nations they have converted the devil – under such names as Old Horny – into a familiar acquaintance not without a certain grim charm of his own. No doubt also there enters into their humour something of the original barbaric attitude towards things. For a primitive people who saw death often and at first hand, and for whom the future world was a vivid reality, that could be *felt*, as it were, in the midnight forest and heard in the roaring storm – for such a people it was no doubt natural to turn the flank of terror by forcing a merry and jovial acquaintance with the unseen world. Such a practice as a wake, and the merrymaking about the corpse, carry us back to the twilight of the world, with the poor savage in his bewildered misery, pretending that his dead still lived. Our funeral with its black trappings and its elaborate ceremonies is the lineal descendant of a merrymaking. Our undertaker is, by evolution, a genial master of ceremonies, keeping things lively at the death-dance. Thus have the ceremonies and the trappings of death been transformed in the course of ages till the forced gaiety is gone, and the black hearse and the gloomy mutes betoken the cold dignity of our despair.

But I fear this article is getting serious. I must apologise.

I was about to say, when I wandered from the point, that there is another form of humour which I am also quite unable to appreciate. This is that particular form of story which may be called, par excellence, the English Anecdote. It always deals with persons of rank and birth, and, except for the exalted nature of the subject itself, is, as far as I can see, absolutely pointless.

This is the kind of thing that I mean.

"His Grace the Fourth Duke of Marlborough was noted for the open-handed hospitality which reigned at Blenheim, the family seat, during his régime. One day on going in to luncheon it was discovered that there were thirty guests present, whereas the table only held covers for twenty-one. 'Oh, well,' said the Duke, not a whit abashed, 'some of us will have to eat standing up.' Everybody, of course, roared with laughter."

My only wonder is that they didn't kill themselves with it. A mere roar doesn't seem enough to do justice to such a story as this.

The Duke of Wellington has been made the storm-centre of three generations of wit of this sort. In fact the typical Duke of Wellington story has been reduced to a thin skeleton such as this:

"A young subaltern once met the Duke of Wellington coming out of Westminster Abbey. 'Good morning, your Grace,' he said, 'rather a wet morning.' 'Yes,' said the Duke, with a very rigid bow, 'but it was a damn sight wetter, sir, on the morning of Waterloo.' The young subaltern, rightly rebuked, hung his head."

Nor is it only the English who sin in regard to anecdotes.

One can indeed make the sweeping assertion that the telling of stories as a mode of amusing others, ought to be kept within strict limits. Few people realise how extremely difficult it is to tell a story so as to reproduce the real fun of it – to "get it over" as the actors say. The mere "facts" of a story seldom make it funny. It needs the right words, with every word in its proper place. Here and there, perhaps once in a hundred times a story turns up which needs no telling. The humour of it turns so completely on a sudden twist or incongruity in the dénouement of it that no narrator however clumsy can altogether fumble it.

Take, for example, this well known instance – a story which, in one form or other, everybody has heard.

"George Grossmith, the famous comedian, was once badly run down and went to consult a doctor. It happened that the doctor, though, like everybody else, he had often seen Grossmith on the stage, had never seen him without his make-up and did not know him by sight. He examined his patient, looked at his tongue, felt his pulse and tapped his lungs. Then he shook his head. 'There's nothing wrong with you, sir,' he said, 'except that you're run down from overwork and worry. You need rest and amusement. Take a night off and go and see George Grossmith at the Savoy.'

"'Thank you,' said the patient, 'I *am* George Grossmith.'"

Let the reader please observe that I have purposely told this story all wrongly, just as wrongly as could be, and yet there is something left of it. Will the reader kindly look back to the beginning of it and see for himself just how it ought to be narrated and what obvious error has been made. If he has any particle of the artist in his make-up, he will see at once that the story ought to begin:

"One day a very haggard and nervous looking patient called at the office of a fashionable doctor, etc., etc."

In other words, the chief point of the joke lies in keeping it concealed till the moment when the patient says, "Thank you, I am George Grossmith." But the story is such a good one that it cannot be completely spoiled even when told wrongly. This particular anecdote has been variously told of George Grossmith, Coquelin, Joe Jefferson, John Hare, Cyril Maude, and about sixty others. And I have noticed that there is a certain type of man who, on hearing this story about Grossmith, immediately tells it all back again, putting in the name of somebody else, and goes into new fits of laughter over it, as if the change of name made it brand new.

But few people, I repeat, realise the difficulty of reproducing a humorous or comic effect in its original spirit.

"I saw Harry Lauder last night," said Griggs, a Stock-Exchange friend of mine, as we walked up town together the other day. "He came onto the stage in kilts" (here Griggs started to chuckle) "and he had a slate under his arm" (here Griggs began to laugh quite heartily), "and he said, 'I always like to carry a slate with me' (of course he said it in Scotch, but I can't do the Scotch the way he does it) 'just in case there might be any figures I'd be wanting to put down'" (by this time Griggs was almost suffocated with laughter) – "and he took a little bit of chalk out of his pocket, and he said" (Griggs was now almost hysterical), "'I like to carry a wee bit chalk along because I find the slate is (Griggs was now faint with laughter), "'the slate is – is – not much good without the chalk.'"

Griggs had to stop, with his hand to his side and lean against a lamp post. "I can't, of course, do the Scotch the way Harry Lauder does it," he repeated.

Exactly. He couldn't do the Scotch and he couldn't do the rich mellow voice of Mr. Lauder and the face beaming with merriment, and the spectacles glittering with amusement, and he couldn't do the slate, nor the "wee bit chalk" – in fact he couldn't do any of it. He ought merely to have said, "Harry Lauder," and leaned up against a post and laughed till he had got over it.

Yet in spite of everything, people insist on spoiling conversation by telling stories. I know nothing more dreadful at a dinner table than one of these amateur raconteurs – except perhaps two of them. After about three stories have been told, there falls on the dinner table an uncomfortable silence, in which everybody is aware that everybody else is trying hard to think of another story, and is failing to find it. There is no peace in the gathering again till some man of firm and quiet mind turns to his neighbour and says – "But after all there is no doubt that whether we like it or not prohibition is coming." Then everybody in his heart says, Thank Heaven! and the whole tableful are happy and contented again, till one of the story tellers "thinks of another," and breaks loose.

Worst of all perhaps is the modest story teller who is haunted by the idea that one has heard his story before. He attacks you after this fashion:

"I heard a very good story the other day on the steamer going to Bermuda" – then he pauses with a certain doubt in his face – "but perhaps you've heard this?"

"No, no, I've never been to Bermuda. Go ahead."

"Well, this is a story that they tell about a man who went down to Bermuda one winter to get cured of rheumatism – but you've heard this?"

"No, no."

"Well he had rheumatism pretty bad and he went to Bermuda to get cured of it. And so when he went into the hotel he said to the clerk at the desk – but, perhaps you know this."

"No, no, go right ahead."

"Well, he said to the clerk I want a room that looks out over the sea – but perhaps —"

Now the sensible thing to do is to stop the narrator right at this point. Say to him quietly and firmly, "Yes, I have heard that story. I always liked it ever since it came out in *Titbits* in 1878, and I read it every time I see it. Go on and tell it to me and I'll sit back with my eyes closed and enjoy it."

No doubt the story-telling habit owes much to the fact that ordinary people, quite unconsciously, rate humour very low: I mean, they underestimate the difficulty of "making humour." It would never occur to them that the thing is hard, meritorious and dignified. Because the result is gay and light, they think the process must be. Few people would realise that it is much harder to write one of Owen Seaman's "funny" poems in *Punch* than to write one of the Archbishop of Canterbury's sermons. Mark Twain's *Huckleberry Finn* is a greater work than Kant's *Critique of Pure Reason,* and Charles Dickens' creation of Mr. Pickwick did more for the elevation of the human race – I say it in all seriousness – than Cardinal Newman's *Lead, Kindly Light, Amid the Encircling Gloom.* Newman only cried out for light in the gloom of a sad world. Dickens gave it.

But the deep background that lies behind and beyond what we call humour is revealed only to the few who, by instinct or by effort, have given thought to it. The world's humour, in its best and greatest sense, is perhaps the highest product of our civilisation. One thinks here not of the mere spasmodic effects of the comic artist or the blackface expert of the vaudeville show, but of the really great humour which, once or twice in a generation at best, illuminates and elevates our literature. It is no longer dependent upon the mere trick and quibble of words, or the odd and meaningless incongruities in things that strike us as "funny." Its basis lies in the deeper contrasts offered by life itself: the strange incongruity between our aspiration and our achievement, the eager and fretful anxieties of to-day that fade into nothingness to-morrow, the burning pain and the sharp sorrow that are softened in the gentle retrospect of time, till as we look back upon the course that has been traversed we pass in view the panorama of our lives, as people in old age may recall, with mingled tears and smiles, the angry quarrels of their childhood. And here, in its larger aspect, humour is blended with pathos till the two are one, and represent, as they have in every age, the mingled heritage of tears and laughter that is our lot on earth.

(1916)

The Saving Grace of Humour

Is There Any?

NOW ESPECIALLY, in the distress of war, the familiar reference is made to the saving grace of humour as a consolation in adversity. But I am afraid there's not much in it – I doubt if any saving grace of humour can help us – at any rate not against personal discomfiture.

I recall here, from years back, once hearing an academic colleague of mine say, "Thank Heaven, I can fall back on my sense of humour." He was speaking with the quivering, ruffled dignity of a professor – you know what they're like – after some little academic tiff or dispute, a small, precise man, myopic, over-polite and sensitive as a mimosa plant. "In fact," he added, "I can even afford to laugh about it, ha! ha!"; and he gave an imitation of a man laughing an easy, careless laugh – as nearly as he could register it. If he had a sense of humour I never saw it; he never seemed to get any nearer to it than telling long stories about Talleyrand, at professors' dinner parties. You know the kind. But yet he carried with him the idea that he could always fall back on his sense of humour – like throwing himself into a firemen's net.

Strange, isn't it?, how we always try to have some refuge of this sort, something to fall back upon. An old friend of mine once told me he could always fall back on his classical education. I'd as soon fall back on a cucumber frame as on mine.

Other people fall back on their family. "After all," I heard a mother say to her son, "you can always remember you're an O'Brien." Personally I could see no consolation in that, except that it was easier than trying to remember you were an O'Flaherty.

But so it is, in our sorely beset pilgrimage; we like to have something to fall back upon – a second line of retreat from the slings and arrows. And the belief is familiar, that this refuge can be found in a sense of humour.

The world loves to read stories of how humour sustains people in moments of emergency and in the supreme hour. Thus it is told of the aged Sir Thomas More, beheaded by Henry VIII, that as he went up the steps of the scaffold he leaned on the executioner with the words, "I pray you give me your aid in my going up; as for my coming down I can make shift for myself." It is told of him, presumably on the same occasion, that as he laid his head on the block he moved aside his snow-white beard, "Pity to cut that," he said; "that has not committed treason." In fact the only trouble with these Thomas More stories is that there are getting to be too many of them. Where did I read one the other day that said: Every time that Sir Thomas More was executed he used to have a clean shave. "Pity," he said, "to get my beard spoiled." I felt when I read it that there was something wrong with that story, though it's hard to see just what. Or was it an advertisement, that read: Sir Thomas More said, "I know nothing like Silver-Glass soap; nothing like it for a hasty shave before execution." But I doubt whether in reality Sir Thomas More got much consolation or fun out of any of it. The executioner probably got more than he did. "Certainly," said the executioner, laughing as he swung up the axe, "you are the most humorous gentleman I ever –" chuck!

Such stories of humour in the presence of death, don't go.

Here is Rabelais, for example, saying "I am about to take a leap into the great perhaps!" And here is the story of O. Henry's last hour on which those of us who love his writings have lingered with wistful affection. "Turn up the light," he said, as the room darkened; "I don't want to go home in the dark." Yet this is not humour. This is pathetic, tragic; this is just the mind still functioning in a worn groove, reverting back like Falstaff when he "babbled of green fields." The cold reality of death cannot be exorcised with a joke. . . .

But if you want to see death and danger treated with absolutely unconcerned laughter turn back again to the stories of adventure that you used to read when you were a boy. Open again the pages of *Ned Dashaway,* or *Adventures on the Spanish Main.* See where it reads: "*Warm work, Ned,*" *laughed Captain Bilge, as a volley of grape cleared three men out of the main top.* "*It certainly is,*" *roared Ned, as a volley of cannister swept the bosun and four men off the main-deck.* "*I'll say so too,*" *chuckled the mate, as a round shot bowled him into the lee-scuppers.*

You notice in these stories, now that you can look at them with the eye of experience, that to keep up the laugh they have to avoid all gruesome details of blood and butchery. What happened to the men in the main top? – They got cleared out of it – that's all – and only cleared with "grape"! That's nothing – and the bosun and his crowd? They got swept off the deck. No harm in that – just a sort of "Excuse me, gentlemen, we want to sweep this deck." Reality is very different from that.

Do you remember how good old Mark Twain wrote a book that he called *Joan of Arc* and really thought was Joan of Arc, and wanted to bring in mediaeval hand-to-hand fighting; and he couldn't do it – unconsciously, I mean, he couldn't. He tried to and it came out like this, in a passage meant to describe a fierce and bloody assault: "We had a long and tough piece of work before us, but we carried it through before night, Joan keeping us hard at it."

Kept them *hard at it*, eh? spirited girl. It sounds like a

Missouri paring bee. No, no, there is no humour in the realities of emergency, danger and death.

Nor can I feel that it could in any way soften or redeem the character of bloodthirsty and awful people if they showed a high sense of humour. If I have to think of Ivan the Terrible, I'd rather think of him as Terrible and let it go at that; I don't want him funny. I'd rather take Blackbeard the pirate as straight Blackbeard and not understand that though he made people walk the plank he could always enter into the fun of the thing. I wouldn't think any better of Blackbeard if I heard that he used to roar over the *Pickwick Papers*. This is the principle on which are based those masterpieces of humour, the *Ruthless Rhymes* of the late Captain Harry Graham. The humour of them lies in the ridiculous incongruity as between the actual tragedy and the cheerful unconcern of the spectators. In other words the saving grace of humour, produced, like the parallel lines of Euclid, "ever so far both ways," reveals its weakness by failing to meet. Readers who know the Rhymes already will forgive me for quoting an example:

> My son Augustus in the street one day
> Was feeling quite particularly merry,
> When some one asked him, "What's the quickest way
> To get me out to Highgate Cemetery?"
> "The quickest way?" replied my little Gus,
> And pushed the feller underneath a bus.
> > I will say this about my son,
> > He does enjoy a bit of fun.

But in reality when tragedy steps in, humour moves out. It is too soft a plant, too soft a blossom for such a soil. Humour springs best from happiness, bubbles forth with the champagne around the festive board. A jail is no place for it. It belongs either with happiness, or with the remembrance of bygone happiness, or with that long retrospect into a past so far away that the pain is out of it. "Battles long ago" are different. I can laugh at Jack and the Giant Killer and the Welsh Giant . . . but that's far away.

Yet I admit we have to make a pretense at humour in moments of trial. It is a sort of survival quality that came down with us through the ages that we must take adversity with a smile or a joke. Tell any man that he has lost his job, and his "reaction," as they say in college, will be to make some kind of joke about having lots of time now for golf. In each of us is the dim conception of being a "sport," a survival, I do not doubt, of bygone ages when of necessity courage was the highest virtue. So it is that collectively and singly we still keep up a brave little show of "laughing it off!" of "clink to the Cannikin, clink!" – a whole repertory of little verses saying that we don't care – when our hearts are broken. . . . Yet this is not humour; this is courage that makes a pretense of it.

I spoke of the *Pickwick Papers,* written, as I am sure some one interrupted to remind me, nearly a hundred years after Blackbeard's death. Now there, I admit, that's different. This is humour not as a saving grace for the maker of it, but handed out as salvation, or at least consolation for mankind. All Dickens's humour couldn't save Dickens, save him from his overcrowded life, its sordid and neurotic central tragedy and its premature collapse. But Dickens's humour, and all such humour, has saved or at least greatly served the world.

One thinks of the *Pickwick Papers* – read in all corners of the world, in the loneliness of exile, in the vigil of the sickroom, in the pauses of toil and the breathing spaces of anxiety, and bringing with it at least a respite of escape, a vision of the lanes and hawthorns of England, of the Christmas snow, and the dim sound on the ear of the bugles of coaches. Nothing else is read like that. Civilization's best legacy, thus far, is the world's humour.

In fact on reflection I'll go a little further in regard to this saving grace of humour. It helps to supply for us, in its degree, such reconciliation as we can find for the mystery, the sorrows, the shortcomings of the world we live in, or, say, of life itself. Consolation is hard to find. You recall perhaps the haunting verses, written years ago, that ran, "There, little girl, don't cry." They have broken her dolls, yes, and later on, it will be her heart that is broken, but, "there, little girl, don't cry." It is all that we can say to one another.

Now humour in its highest reach turns on just such feeling as this. It is not funny. It no longer rests on quips of language, the oddities of situation or the incongruities of character – but on the incongruity of life itself. The contrast between the eager fret and anxiety of today, the angers that pass and are forgotten and in retrospect, like children's quarrels, provoke only a smile – this is the basis on which the world's greatest books of humour appeal to us. This mellowed vision even though not interpretation at least contains reconciliation and consolation.

Not that I mean that a person with a sense of humour can sit and chuckle over it all. That is given only to idiots. You can't slap your leg and roar with laughter at how funny it is the Romans are all dead. But at least – well – there's an idea that I am groping for, but as Sir Thomas More would say to the executioner, "Pity to spoil it."

(1942)

Afterword

BY DAVID STAINES

While he was teaching at Upper Canada College in Toronto, Stephen Leacock wrote his first humorous stories. Between 1894 and 1897 he published twenty-five pieces, including "My Financial Career" and "The Awful Fate of Melpomenus Jones." Looking back later, he reflected on his failure to know at that time "where to find material for literary work. It seemed to me that my life as a resident schoolmaster was so limited and uninteresting that there was nothing in it to write about. Later on, when I had learned how, I was able to turn back to it and write it up with great pecuniary satisfaction. But that was after I had learned how to let nothing get past me."

At this early stage in his literary career, Leacock did not realize that humour originates in the humorist's own world of experiences. "No matter how restricted your life is," he would later advise would-be writers, "there is plenty of material in it and around you to write about. Your father, for instance, couldn't you do something with him? . . . or, if not your father, then, at any rate, Uncle Joe, because everybody says he's a regular character."

After 1897 Leacock left high-school teaching, pursued doctoral studies at the University of Chicago, accepted a teaching position in the Department of Political Science and Economics of McGill University, and published the textbook *Elements of Political Science* (1906). That scholarly work, he recalled many years after, "had a peculiar effect" on him. "I found that again and again I wanted to put something funny into it. I was sure I could describe much better the nature of British government if I were allowed to put in a dialogue between the Keeper of the Swans and the Clerk of the Cheque, or the Master of the Bloodhounds. I refer, of course, to all those queer officials in England who sound like a winning hand at poker. In them really lies the essence of British government, British character, and British success."

Although *Elements of Political Science* met with critical and commercial success, Leacock determined to return to his beloved avocation, the writing of humour. He gathered together nineteen of his early pieces, added twenty-one new stories, and published them privately in 1910 under the title *Literary Lapses*. The book's immediate popularity, and its subsequent and successful publication the following year in England and the United States, established Leacock's reputation as a humorist, thus complementing his reputation as a political economist. From 1910 until his death in 1944, he published a book of humour almost every year, and he came to be acknowledged both at home and abroad as the finest humorist in the English-speaking world.

Leacock once defined humour as "the kindly contemplation of the incongruities of life, and the artistic expression thereof." Even his earliest stories reflect the always apparent contrasts between life as it might be and as it is, between an ideal world and ordinary reality, between our aspirations and our achievements. His fiction portrays these discrepancies with kindness, compassion, and sympathy, with bemused and caring understanding.

The world of Leacock's humour is the world of the "regular character," the average individual caught in the dilemmas of daily existence, "the eager and fretful anxieties of today that fade into nothingness tomorrow." This person is the customer in the bank, making his first – and – last deposit; Melpomenus Jones trying hopelessly to extricate himself from awkward situations; the townspeople of Mariposa enduring yet again the sinking of the Mariposa Belle; the patient trapped in the dentist's chair; the golfer trying to excuse his poor performance. The innocence of such people can become the gullibility of Peter Spillikins, the incompetence of the hopeless spy, or the credulity of the victims of mercenary spiritualists. Nevertheless, Leacock's sympathy always rests with the forlorn individual beleaguered by the demands of social conventions and institutions.

Sometimes the kindly contemplation becomes less kindly, the irony, for example, of "The Marine Excursion of the Knights of Pythias" from *Sunshine Sketches of a Little Town* giving way to the less kindly satire of "The Love Story of Mr. Peter Spillikins" from *Arcadian Adventures with the Idle Rich.* For Leacock the economist, the abuse and misuse of wealth, a constant theme in his non-fiction, sees in some of his humorous stories an unkind or even angry satire replacing a more usual sympathetic irony. Such instances are rare, but remind us of the social critic who always stands behind the humorist.

Leacock the humorist was also Leacock the parodist, setting aside "the kindly contemplation" of life for an equally "kindly" contemplation of literature. His second volume of humour, *Nonsense Novels*, which always remained one of his favourite books, had, as he happily confessed in 1935, "no small vogue in the last quarter of a century. The ten stories that make it up are not parodies of any particular stories or of any particular author. They reproduce types." Leacockian parodies are affectionate tributes to earlier literary genres, for example, "Gertrude the Governess: or, Simple Seventeen" evokes the historical novel and "Buggam Grange" the ghost story. But in reproducing the original genres, he also recognizes their inherent limitations. The parody is, wrote Leacock, "a protest against the over-sentimentality, or the over-reputation of the original." Leacock the parodist, never irreverent to his literary models, nevertheless makes their extravagances a source of laughter: "The essential point is the use of parody as corrective to over-sentiment, of humour as a relief from pain, or humour as a consolation against the short-comings of life itself."

For Leacock, humour is, above all else, consolation, the only comfort available in this lonely existence. Born in Victorian England, Leacock was a product of his time, knowing the Victorian decline in religious belief and turning to humour as a possible if temporary comfort: "Humour in a world of waning beliefs remains like Hope still left at the bottom of Pandora's box when all of the evils of the gods flew out from it upon the world."

"Each of us in life is a prisoner," Leacock wrote in *Humour: Its Theory and Technique* (1935). "The past offers us, as it were a door of escape. We are set and bound in our confined lot. Outside, somewhere, is eternity; outside, somewhere, is infinity. We seek to reach into it and the pictured past seems to afford to us an outlet of escape." But there is no real escape from our confined lot, except through the laughter prompted by a comic understanding of the human condition. "In retrospect all our little activities are but as nothing, all that we do has in it a touch of the pathetic, and even our sins and wickedness and crime are easily pardoned in the realization of their futility."

Confronted with this seeming nothingness, Leacock, a true modern, found little comfort in faith or religion. In 1934 he wrote to his son, advising him not "to be confirmed until you have given much more thought to what it implies than you have probably done up till now." Confirmation demands that the faithful "express an honest and honorable belief, without equivocation, in a lot of things which I am apt to think you don't believe, and which, personally, I reject." To his son he came close to expressing his personal non-creed: "Those who can believe these things are happy in the comfort of them, and die happy in them . . . But those of us who cannot believe them must find our salvation elsewhere. It is for you to decide. Unbelief is a burden, but the pretence of belief, hypocrisy, is death to all that is decent in you."

Humour is consolation, comfort, perhaps even salvation. In its highest meaning humour "finds its basis in the incongruity of life itself, the contrast between the fretting cares and the petty sorrows of the day and the long mystery of the tomorrow. Here laughter and tears become one, and humour becomes the contemplation and interpretation of our life."

At the end of "Fifty Cents' Worth," Fred can offer his wife only the consoling words, "Don't cry, dear. Don't cry." The narrator closes the story: "And with this first and last of human consolations on his lips, he leaves her to herself." Fred's words, Leacock acknowledges in "The Saving Grace of Humour," are "all that we can say to one another."

The love expressed in the words "Don't cry" informs Leacock's comic vision. Humour, he believed, "helps to supply for us, in its degree, such reconciliation as we can find for the mystery, the sorrows, the shortcomings we live in, or, say, of life itself. Consolation is hard to find."

Leacock's avocation, the writing of humour, had in time become his vocation – thus relieving life's burdens through the consolation and comfort of laughter.

BY STEPHEN LEACOCK

Adventures of the Far North:
A Chronicle of the Frozen Seas (1914)
The Dawn of Canadian History: A Chronicle of Aboriginal
Canada and the Coming of the White Man (1914)
The Mariner of St. Malo:
A Chronicle of the Voyages of Jacques Cartier (1914)
Mackenzie, Baldwin, Lafontaine, Hincks (1926)
Lincoln Frees the Slaves (1934)
The British Empire:
Its Structure, Its History, Its Strength (1940)
Canada: The Foundations of Its Future (1941)
Our Heritage of Liberty: Its Origin, Its Achievement, Its Crisis:
A Book for War Time (1942)
Montreal: Seaport and City (1942)
Canada and the Sea (1944)

HUMOUR

Literary Lapses (1910)
Nonsense Novels (1911)
Sunshine Sketches of a Little Town (1912)
Behind the Beyond and Other Contributions to Human
Knowledge (1913)
Arcadian Adventures with the Idle Rich (1914)
Moonbeams from the Larger Lunacy (1915)
Further Foolishness:
Sketches and Satires on the Follies of the Day (1916)
Frenzied Fiction (1918)
The Hohenzollerns in America; With the Bolsheviks in Berlin,
and Other Impossibilities (1919)
Winsome Winnie, and Other New Nonsense Novels (1920)
My Discovery of England (1922)
College Days (1923)
Over the Footlights (1923)
The Garden of Folly (1924)

Winnowed Wisdom (1926)
Short Circuits (1928)
The Iron Man and the Tin Woman,
with Other Such Futurities (1929)
Wet Wit and Dry Humour:
Distilled from the Pages of Stephen Leacock (1931)
The Dry Pickwick and Other Incongruities (1932)
Afternoons in Utopia: Tales of the New Time (1932)
Hellements of Hickonomics in Hiccoughs of Verse Done in Our
Social Planning Mill (1936)
Funny Pieces: A Book of Random Sketches (1936)
Here Are My Lectures (1937)
Model Memoirs, and Other Sketches
from Simple to Serious (1938)
My Remarkable Uncle and Other Sketches (1942)
Happy Stories Just to Laugh At (1943)
Last Leaves (1945)

LITERARY CRITICISM
Essays and Literary Studies (1916)
Humour: Its Theory and Technique (1935)
The Greatest Pages of American Humor (1936)
Humour and Humanity: An Introduction to the Study of
Humour (1937)
How to Write (1943)

POLITICAL SCIENCE
Elements of Political Science (1906)
The Unsolved Riddle of Social Justice (1920)
My Discovery of the West: A Discussion of
East and West in Canada (1937)
While There Is Time:
The Case against Social Catastrophe (1945)